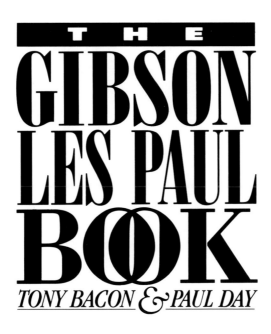

THE
GIBSON
LES PAUL
BOOK

TONY BACON & PAUL DAY

The Gibson Les Paul Book
A complete history of Les Paul guitars
By Tony Bacon & Paul Day

GPI BOOKS
Miller Freeman Inc.
San Francisco

Published in the UK by Balafon Books, an imprint of Outline Press Ltd,
115J Cleveland Street, London W1P 5PN, England.

First American Edition
Published in the United States by the GPI Books Division
of Miller Freeman Inc., 600 Harrison Street, San Francisco,
California 94107
Publishers of Guitar Player and Bass Player magazines

ISBN 0-87930-289-5

Library of Congress Card Number 93-78339

Printed in Hong Kong

Editor: Roger Cooper
Art Director: Nigel Osborne
Design: Sally Stockwell

99 00 01 02 8 7 6 5

CONTENTS

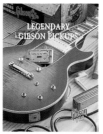

LEGENDARY GIBSON PICKUPS

"The Fretless Wonder"
THE INCOMPARABLE
LES PAUL CUSTOM GUITAR

INTRODUCTION

The Les Paul model was Gibson's first solidbody electric guitar. Since its debut in 1952, thousands upon thousands of Les Paul instruments have poured out of Gibson's factories, from the earliest attempts built in Michigan to the latest models made in the company's plant in Tennessee.

Until now, no single book has documented the fascinating development of Gibson's Les Paul guitars. We examine the original collaboration between the traditional Gibson company, best known back then for archtop acoustic instruments, and the brilliant musician Les Paul, hugely successful in the 1950s as an inventive guitarist in a pop duo with vocalist Mary Ford. We explain why Gibson let the Les Paul guitars drop from production in the early 1960s, and how a surge in interest sparked by guitarists like Eric Clapton in the middle of the decade forced the company to re-introduce the Les Paul models in 1968. And we explore the modern Gibson company's interpretation of the Les Paul designs in the midst of changes in ownership, a factory closure, altered production methods and a gradually evolving attitude to the re-issue of classic models.

The Gibson Les Paul Book is the first wide-ranging study of these important models. We explain and describe the guitars of the 1980s and 1990s as well as the classic early Les Pauls, and analyze the circumstances which led to the often criticized models of the 1970s. We have conducted fresh interviews with leading Gibson employees both past and present to inform our story, and present a host of specially-commissioned full-color photographs of fine guitars and rarely seen memorabilia. Rounding off the book is a comprehensive reference section listing in detail every Gibson Les Paul model from 1952 to 1993, plus concise information to assist in identifying and dating. This is the book that everyone interested in Gibson's Les Paul guitars has been waiting for, and we hope you enjoy it.

TONY BACON & PAUL DAY, ENGLAND, MAY 1993

"We in the industry know that Les Paul is a real guy, but there's a lot of young kids who think that 'Les Paul' is just a guitar."
Henry Juskiewicz, *CURRENTLY PRESIDENT, GIBSON GUITAR CORP.*

"L5 models, Super 400s, banjos, mandolins, acoustics. . . that's what Gibson was known for. And all of a sudden here comes this strange *thing.*"
Bruce Bolen, *GIBSON EMPLOYEE 1967-1986, on the birth of the Les Paul model.*

"A great deal of mythology has grown up about something that came essentially from a nice bunch of folks in the Midwest doing the best job they could, paying attention to what they thought mattered, and not caring about much other stuff."
Tim Shaw, *GIBSON EMPLOYEE 1978-1992, on Gibson in the 1950s.*

"People like the imperfections as well as the perfections of the old guitars."
J T Riboloff, *GIBSON EMPLOYEE SINCE 1987.*

"We didn't know if [the Les Paul] was going to catch on. But it did."
Ted McCarty, *PRESIDENT OF GIBSON 1950-1966.*

"I never found a product I loved as much as those Gibson guitars. You took an ugly piece of wood and you made something beautiful."
Stan Rendell, *PRESIDENT OF GIBSON 1968-1976.*

"Mr Berlin [the head of Gibson's parent company] said, Les I gotta ask you something. In your wildest dreams, did you ever think that the Gibson Les Paul guitar would become this big? And I said, Of course! I believed in it all the way through."
Les Paul, *MUSICIAN AND INVENTOR.*

THIS PAGE, ABOVE: In Gibson's Kalamazoo factory around 1955 Les Paul holds a special flat-topped Les Paul Custom model being presented to him by Gibson president Ted McCarty. A smiling worker looks on, and standing behind the guitar rack is McCarty's assistant, John Huis, who was in charge of production.

THIS PAGE, LEFT: This 1960 Les Paul Sunburst – once owned by Joe Walsh, now by Alan Rogan – has a highly desirable 'flamed' top.

OPPOSITE PAGE, TOP ROW: This trade ad from 1957 (left) stresses the marketing potential of Les Paul & Mary Ford's regular appearances on TV and radio with Gibson Les Paul guitars always close by. Maurice Berlin (center) and his CMI company acquired Gibson in 1944. Les Paul (right) often modified the instruments Gibson sent him.

OPPOSITE PAGE, MIDDLE ROW: Ted McCarty (left) was president of Gibson from 1950 to 1966. A promo shot from 1952 (right) has Les & Mary apparently sitting astride a prototype Les Paul model: it has a tailpiece from an archtop guitar and experimental pickups.

OPPOSITE PAGE, BOTTOM ROW: "They're Tops..." reads this 1950s ad (left), as Gibson are quick to connect Les Paul & Mary Ford's sensational chart-topping success with their new Gibson Les Paul guitars. Les Paul is pictured (right) on a **Guitar Player** magazine cover from 1977 with one of his developmental 'Log' electric guitars of the 1940s.

LES PAUL was born Lester William Polfus in Waukesha, Wisconsin, in June 1915. He started his professional life as a talented, teenage guitarist; by the age of 17 he was broadcasting on local radio stations, playing country under the name of Rhubarb Red and adding R&B and jazz to his expanding repertoire.

It soon became clear that his ambition would not rest solely in playing. Lester had an apparently natural technical ability, which he applied not only to music but also to making his own bits and pieces of instrumental and electronic gadgetry. Later he would be lucky enough to come up with several musical inventions in the right place and at the right time, which means that historians today worry about whether to call Les Paul a musician or an inventor. They generally settle for both.

Like a number of performers at the time, the young Lester soon became interested in the idea of amplifying his guitar. He recollects that in his early teens he tried to amplify an acoustic instrument by "jabbing a phonograph pickup into the guitar". Soon afterwards he says he appropriated an old telephone mouthpiece along with his parents' radio to bring his unaccompanied guitar to the attention of the audience at a local roadhouse gig.

Others were thinking along similar if less extreme lines. In the early 1930s the Rickenbacker guitar company in California was among the first of a number of smaller makers to market an electric version of the popular 'lap steel' guitar. This was a variety played on the lap with a steel bar sliding across the raised strings.

Around this time companies such as Rickenbacker, National and others also began to sell instruments with electric pickups and associated controls built into normal 'Spanish' archtop acoustic guitars. By the middle of the 1930s Gibson, of Kalamazoo, Michigan, one of the most successful guitar-making companies, had entered this 'amplified acoustic' market with their ES150 model and associated amplifier, as had their biggest competitor, Epiphone.

Meanwhile, Lester Polfus had permanently adopted a suitably shortened version of his name – Les Paul. In the late 1930s Paul's new jazz-based trio was broadcasting out

of New York on the Fred Waring radio show and with Ben Bernie's Big Band. At first Paul was playing a guitar made by Gibson (he is pictured in their 1937 catalogue as Rhubarb Red, playing a Super 400 model, although he favoured an L5). Later he switched to Epiphone, a company based in New York and set up around 1910 by a guitar maker of Greek extraction, Epaminondas Stathopoulo. (Stathopoulo's first name was generally shortened to Epi; add the Greek word for sound and you have Epiphone.)

Les Paul's Log

Les Paul exercised his curiosity for electric instruments and his flair for technical experimentation by adapting and modifying his Epiphone guitar. He tells a story now of how he used to go into the empty Epiphone factory on weekends, probably around 1940, to fiddle with what he called his 'log' guitar. "Every Sunday I went there and worked. . . Epiphone said, What the hell is it? And I said, It's 'the log', a solidbody guitar."

The 'log' nickname was derived from a 4in x 4in solid block of pine which Paul had inserted between the sawn halves of the dismembered body. Using some metal brackets Paul re-joined the neck to the pine 'log', onto which he mounted a couple of crude home-made pickups. A little later he modified a second and third Epiphone, which he called his 'clunkers', this time chopping up the bodies to add metal strengthening braces, and again topped with Paul's own pickups. Despite their makeshift origins, the semi-solid 'log' and the modified 'clunker' Epiphones often accompanied Les Paul on stage and in recording studios throughout the 1940s and into the early 1950s.

Paul was not alone in his investigations. Several unconnected explorations into the possibility of a solidbody electric guitar were being undertaken elsewhere in America at this time, not least at the Californian workshops of Rickenbacker, National, Bigsby and Fender.

The idea of the solidbody electric was appealing: it would dispose of the involved construction of an acoustic guitar, and instead use a body made of solid wood or some other rigid material to support the strings and pickups. This solid construction would curtail the annoying feedback produced by amplified acoustic guitars. It would also reduce the body's interference with the guitar's overall tone, and thus more accurately reproduce and sustain the sound of the strings.

During the 1940s, Paul decided to take his 'log' idea to a major company, to see if he could generate interest in its commercial potential. He decided, accurately as it turned out, that Epiphone would not continue in their present form as a strong force in the guitar world. He remembers his succinct calculation: "Gibson was the biggest in the business, and that's where I wanted to go."

FROM ORVILLE TO MAURICE

The Gibson company was certainly big, and undoubtedly successful. Orville Gibson had been born in 1856, the son of a British immigrant to the United States, and began making stringed musical instruments in Kalamazoo, Michigan, probably by the 1890s. His unusual and effective use of carved tops, backs and sides for his guitars and mandolins drew attention, and in 1902 the successful maker officially formed the first Gibson company. The Gibson set-up rapidly grew in stature and gained an enviable reputation among musicians for some fine, attractive instruments, with Gibson mandolins in particular achieving wide popularity.

But the guitar too began to grow in importance during the 1920s and 1930s, and it was essential that any company demanding attention among guitarists should be seen as inventive and forward-thinking in this vital new area. Gibson obliged with many six-string innovations, including the adjustable truss-rod for neck strengthening (seen as obligatory on today's guitars). Thanks to the creativity of gifted employees like Lloyd Loar, Gibson also established individual landmarks such as the L5 of the early 1920s. With its novel f-holes and 'floating' pickguard, this model virtually defined the look and sound of the early archtop acoustic guitar. It was played in a variety of musical styles, none more appealing than the 'parlour jazz' epitomised by the

incomparable Eddie Lang (a strong influence on Les Paul's style, in fact).

As players demanded more volume from their guitars, Gibson dutifully increased the size of their products, introducing in the mid 1930s the superb, huge archtop Super 400 guitar, along with 'jumbo' flat-top acoustics such as the impressive J200 model.

A controlling interest in Gibson had been bought in 1944 by the Chicago Musical Instrument Company (or 'CMI'), which had been founded some 25 years earlier in Chicago, Illinois by Maurice H Berlin. Under the new ownership, Berlin thus became the boss of Gibson's parent company. Gibson's general manager Guy Hart stayed on, while John Adams, president since the company's formation in 1902, resigned. Gibson's manufacturing base remained at the original factory, purpose-built in 1917 at Kalamazoo, an industrial and commercial center in a farming area, roughly equidistant from Detroit and Chicago. The latter city was the location for Gibson's new sales and administration headquarters at CMI.

It was around 1946 that Paul took his crude 'log' to Maurice Berlin at CMI in Chicago, with the intention of convincing him to market such a guitar. No doubt with all the courtesy that a pressurized city businessman could muster, the boss of Gibson showed Les Paul the door. "They laughed at the guitar," Paul remembers.

CROSBY CROONS, PAUL RECORDS

Over the next few years, Les Paul became famous. During World War II he'd been in the Armed Forces Radio Service, operating out of their HQ in Hollywood and entertaining the troops. Among the singers he backed was Bing Crosby. After the war Paul played prominent guitar on Crosby's hit 'It's Been A Long Long Time' (1945), which was credited to Bing Crosby With The Les Paul Trio, bringing Paul to a wider audience.

"What Les does to a guitar is I imagine exactly what a guitar likes to have done to it," said Crosby, introducing Paul as a guitar-playing guest on *The Bing Crosby Radio Show* in 1947. Crosby showed a keen interest in new recording developments and became an early user of tape

9

Gold-top 1952 (right)
This guitar is from the very first year of production of the Gibson Les Paul. Note that on the distinctive, large 'trapeze' tailpiece the strings are wrapped underneath the bridge bar. This unsatisfactory arrangement lasted only until 1953. There are also a number of details about this example which suggest that it comes from one of the earliest production runs of this first gold-top type: the Gibson logo has the dot of the 'i' joined to the G, rarely seen on 1952 instruments; the fingerboard is unbound, unlike most gold-tops; and the bridge pickup has screws in opposite corners, whereas most are like the neck pickup.

10

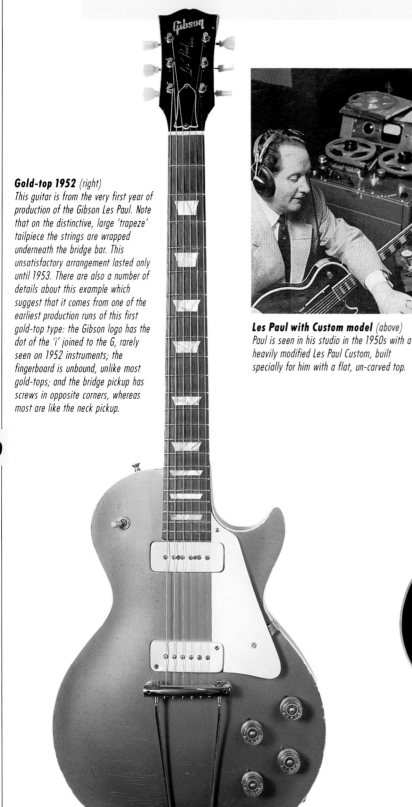

Les Paul with Custom model (above)
Paul is seen in his studio in the 1950s with a heavily modified Les Paul Custom, built specially for him with a flat, un-carved top.

Custom 1956 (above)
The second Les Paul model to appear (in 1954), this handsome black and gold variation on the basic design had a new 'alnico' pickup at the neck.

Gold-top ad 1953 *(left)*
This is one of the first press advertisements for "the newest Gibson guitar", the Les Paul gold-top. The company described their new "sensation" as a "unique and exciting innovation in the fretted instrument field". During the whole of 1953 Gibson sold a little over 2200 gold-tops, easily the model's most successful year in the 1950s.

John Lee Hooker *(above)*
Evidently the bluesman held an early gold-top Les Paul model at least once. A remarkably un-modern sounding blues guitarist, Hooker often used open tunings for his earlier solo performances, but by the time of this 1950s shot he was with a band.

Gold-top 1952 *(left)*
Left-handed players have two basic options. They can turn over a right-handed guitar, re-arranging the strings if they wish; or they can buy special 'reversed' left-handed guitars, which *have always been made in smaller quantities. This first-year gold-top lefty in excellent condition is therefore something of a rarity.*

11

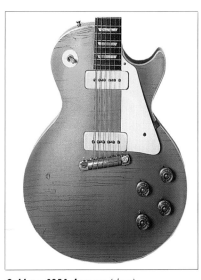

Gold-top 1954 close-up *(above)*
It soon became clear that the gold-top's original 'trapeze' bridge/tailpiece, combined with the guitar's shallow neck pitch, was impractical. During 1953 the model began to be fitted with a one-piece bar-shaped combined bridge/tailpiece, as seen on this example. The unit is often nicknamed a 'stud' type thanks to the two metal studs used to secure it into the top of the guitar.

recording machines for his radio show. Crosby encouraged Paul to build a studio into the garage of the guitarist's home in Hollywood, California.

It was in this small home studio that Paul hit upon some effective recording techniques – at first using discs, and soon afterwards tape. Paul's method was to build up multiple layers of instruments by using two recording machines. He would add new material to an existing recording at each pass of the tape, a system he'd developed on the road as a means of playing along with himself. Paul could also vary the tape-speed to produce impossibly high and fast guitar passages. With this homegrown technology, and later with the true sound-on-sound facilities afforded by a single, modified tape recorder, Paul managed to create on tape a huge, magical orchestra of massed guitars playing catchy instrumental tunes.

Les Paul and his 'New Sound' was signed to Capitol Records, and the first release, 'Lover', became a number 21 hit in 1948. But Paul was not alone: singer Patti Page scored a hit the same year with 'Confess', using similar recording tricks to create a whole choir from her voice. A couple of years later she had greater success with 'The Tennessee Waltz', outselling Les Paul's version of the same song in the US charts.

LES PAUL & MARY FORD

Les Paul became a big recording star, but after a long break to recover from a bad car accident he found even greater popularity when he added vocalist Mary Ford to his act. Paul had known Ford (real name Colleen Summers) since 1945, but an official liaison didn't occur until 1949. Their marriage (Paul's second) took place in December, and the following year the duo released their first joint record, 'Cryin''/'Dry My Tears'. Guitars and now voices too were given the multiple recording treatment, and big hits followed for Les Paul & Mary Ford. These hit records included 'The Tennessee Waltz' (which went to number 6 in the US charts in 1950), 'How High The Moon' (to number 1 in 1951), 'The World is Waiting for the Sunrise' (number 2 in 1951), 'Tiger Rag' (number 2, 1952), 'Bye Bye Blues' (number 5,

1953), 'Vaya Con Dios' (number 1, 1953), 'I'm Sitting on Top of the World' (number 10, 1953), and 'I'm A Fool To Care' (number 6, 1954).

The duo performed a host of personal appearances and concerts, and they were heard on NBC Radio's *Les Paul Show* every week for six months during 1949 and 1950. They starred in a networked TV series *Les Paul & Mary Ford At Home*, which began in 1953 and ran for years, filmed at their new house in Mahwah, New Jersey. As the 1950s got underway Les Paul & Mary Ford, 'America's Musical Sweethearts', were huge stars.

THE FENDER FIRST

In 1950 a small Californian company which made amplifiers and electric lap-steel guitars launched onto an unsuspecting market the world's first commercially available solidbody electric 'Spanish' guitar. This innovative musical instrument was originally called the Fender Esquire or Broadcaster, soon renamed the Fender Telecaster.

Fender's initial burst of activity did not instantly convert guitarists everywhere to the solidbody cause. At first, the company's electrics were used by a handful of country players and western-swing guitarists, principally from areas local to the company's workshop in Fullerton, California. But slowly the word spread, and Fender's rise to the top of the electric guitar market had begun. Such a success, even if modest at first, did not go unnoticed among other guitar makers – including Gibson over in Kalamazoo.

Ted McCarty had joined Gibson in March 1948, having worked at the Wurlitzer organ company for the previous 12 years, and in 1950 he was made president of Gibson. McCarty recalls that Maurice Berlin, head of Gibson's parent company CMI in Chicago, had appointed him to improve Gibson's operational performance, which had been suffering since World War II. Gibson had suspended most musical instrument production during the war and had undertaken government electronics work for radar installations, earning the company three Army & Navy 'E' awards.

McCarty says that Gibson was finding it hard in the

12

post-war years to get back into full-scale guitar production. His first tasks when he joined were to increase the effectiveness of supervision, bolster efficiency, and widen internal communication. "I went there on the 15th of March 1948," he remembers, "and we lost money in March, we lost money in April, we made money in May, and we made it for the next 18 years that I was there."

By 1950 Gibson's electric guitar range numbered seven models, from the ES125 at $97.50, through the ES140, ES150, ES175, ES300 and ES350, up to the ES5 at $375. Of course, these were all of the carved-top, hollowbody, f-holed, 'amplified acoustic' variety.

Then along came the Fender solidbody electric. McCarty remembers the reaction at Gibson: "We were watching what Fender was doing, realizing that he was gaining popularity in the West. I watched him and watched him, and said we've got to get into that business. We are giving him a free run, he's the only one making that kind of guitar with that real shrill sound which the country and Western boys liked. It was becoming popular. We talked it over and decided, let's make one. . .

"So we started out to make a solidbody for ourselves. We had a lot to learn about the solidbody guitar. It's different to the acoustic. Built differently, sounds different, responds differently."

Ted McCarty suggests that Gibson started work on its own solidbody guitar project soon after the appearance of Fender's Broadcaster in late 1950, and that McCarty and the company's top engineers were involved in the project. "We designed the guitars. And we started trying to learn something about a solidbody guitar," McCarty says. "I was working with the rest of the engineers and we would sit down, like in a think tank, and we would talk about this guitar: let's do this, let's try that."

When pressed on exactly how many people were involved in the design of this instrument, which was to become the Gibson Les Paul, McCarty says, "Maybe there were four of us. Myself, plus John Huis [McCarty's number two, heading up production], one of the fellows in charge of the wood department, and one of the guitar

players in final assembly." McCarty also mentions Gibson employees Julius Bellson and Wilbur Marker as being "in on this thing," and it's probable that Gibson's salespeople were consulted at various stages via sales manager Clarence Havenga. McCarty continues: "We eventually came up with a guitar that was attractive, and as far as we were concerned it had the tone, it had the resonance, and it also had the sustain – but not too much. To get to that point took us about a year."

Still none of the other guitar-making companies were showing any obvious interest in following Fender's lead into the market for mass-produced solidbody guitars. "Their attitude was: forget it, because anyone with a band-saw and a router can make a solidbody guitar," says McCarty.

"Anyway, we thought we had the guitar, and now we needed an excuse to make it. So I got to thinking. . . at that time Les Paul and Mary Ford were riding very high, they were probably the number one vocal team in the United States. They were earning a million dollars a year. And knowing Les and Mary I decided maybe I ought to show this guitar to them."

RETURN OF THE BROOMSTICK GUY

Paul's recollection is different. He says that Gibson had first contacted him early in 1951, soon after Fender started making their solidbody electric. He remembers that Maurice Berlin, boss of Gibson's parent company, CMI, told his second-in-command Marc Carlucci to get in touch with the fellow with the strange 'log' guitar whom they'd seen briefly back in the 1940s. "They said, Find that guy with the broomstick with the pickups on it," Paul laughs. "They came round right away, soon as they heard what Fender was doing. And I said well, you guys are a little bit behind the times, but OK, let's go."

Paul told Stephen K Peeples, who in 1991 compiled the booklet for a CD box-set of Paul's Capitol recordings, that after Gibson contacted him about their interest in developing a solidbody electric, a meeting was set up at CMI headquarters in Chicago. Present were "Berlin, Carlucci and CMI's attorney, Marv Henrickson, who also represented Les," wrote Peeples, and continued: "They

Factory shot c1956 *(above)*
Here we see the earliest stage in the
life of a Les Paul Junior. A worker at
the Gibson factory in Kalamazoo
maneuvers a basic wooden block to cut
out the shape of the Junior's body,
which will remain flat-topped. Note the
two holes drilled for control shafts.

Gibson catalog 1956 *(right)*
An early appearance in company
literature for the new Les Paul Special
model, combining "the features that
have made the Les Paul Model
famous" with "a moderate price".

**OUTSTANDING
VALUE IN A SOLID BODY GUITAR**

The new LES PAUL SPECIAL solid body Electric Spanish
Cutaway Guitar incorporates the features that have
made the Les Paul Model famous—tone, versatility, slen-
der neck and low, fast action—with a moderate price.
The appearance is rich and attractive . . . solid Honduras
mahogany body and neck finished in limed mahogany
shading . . . contrasting brown Royalite pickguard and
unit covers . . . nickel plated parts . . . 22 frets, bound rosewood fingerboard with pearl dot inlays.

Other features of the Les Paul Special: Two powerful Gibson pickups with separate tone and volume controls for
each; Alnico magnets and individually adjustable polepieces for each string; two position toggle switch activates
either or both pickups; unique combination metal bridge
and tailpiece, adjustable horizontally and vertically; individual Kluson machine heads; adjustable Gibson Truss
Rod neck construction; padded, adjustable leather strap.

Les Paul Special Solid Body Electric Spanish Cutaway Guitar

Cases for Above Instrument: 535 Faultless, 115 Challenge

Junior 1956 *(below)*
Introduced in 1954, the Junior was Gibson's first attempt to make a cheaper Les Paul model. The guitar was aimed at beginners, and/or players on a budget, and featured a single pickup, an un-carved top, and the company's traditional sunburst finish. The frugality of the Junior model was underlined by the simple dot position markers set into an unbound fingerboard.

Gibson catalog 1920s *(right)*
The idea of 'junior' instruments was not a new one at Gibson. This brochure, issued some 30 years before the Les Paul Junior, announces "characteristic Gibson quality at popular prices".

TV 1957 *(above)*
This guitar, a Junior with a beige coloured finish, was given the honor of a separate model name, the Les Paul TV. Presumably this was to capitalize on Les Paul & Mary Ford's TV show of the 1950s, a regular showcase for Gibson's guitars.

15

Special 1957 *(above)*
The Les Paul Special was launched in 1955, effectively a two-pickup version of the Junior. It adopted the Junior's un-carved top, but gained fingerboard binding, the same beige finish as the TV model, and was located toward the bottom of the Les Paul pricelist. The shape of the Junior, TV and Special bodies was later changed (for photographs of the redesigned models, turn to pages 22 and 23).

Gibson catalog 1957 *(left)*
This page features the Junior and TV models, the latter with what Gibson termed their "limed mahogany" finish.

finalized their deal, and hammered out the specifics of the new guitar's design. Then, the research and development began in earnest."

PROTOTYPE PAUL

McCarty continues with his story of how he came to show the first prototype of the Gibson Les Paul guitar to Paul. McCarty and Paul's business manager, Phil Braunstein, took the prototype to where Les and Mary were staying at a friend's hunting lodge in Stroudsburg, Pennsylvania, near the Delaware Water Gap park – this was probably in 1951. They were there together with Ford's sister Carol and her husband Wally Kamin, a bass-playing chum of Paul's, and had come to record, taking advantage of the lodge's quiet, isolated position. McCarty says that his intention was to interest Paul in publicly playing the new guitar in return for a royalty on sales – an arrangement generally referred to now as an endorsement deal. Paul also recalls that the hunting lodge in Stroudsburg was where he saw the first prototype of what became the Gibson Les Paul.

McCarty remembers that Paul loved the prototype, saying to Ford, "I think we ought to join them, what do you think?" and that she said she liked it too. Neither McCarty nor Paul can remember for sure, but the prototype was probably very similar to the eventual production model, except that it most likely had a normal Gibson tailpiece of the period (as for example on a Gibson ES350) with a separate bridge.

An agreement was reached that very night, says McCarty: he and Les Paul and Phil Braunstein sat down and worked out a contract. First they decided on the royalty Gibson would pay for every Les Paul guitar sold. Paul says his royalty on Les Paul models was five per cent. The term of the contract was set at five years.

McCarty remembers: "Phil, Les's business manager, said I want one paragraph in there: Les Paul had to agree that he would not play any guitar other than a Gibson in public during the life of the contract. If in the fourth year he appeared playing a Gretsch, say, it would cancel the whole thing, he wouldn't get a dime."

Braunstein explained that this was to save on tax commitments, and to assure money for Paul and Ford when their income from records and concerts may have waned in later years. McCarty says there was also a clause in the contract stating that Paul should act as a consultant to Gibson. "We agreed that night. We each had a copy, wrote it out long-hand. Les could take it to his attorney and I could take it to ours, and if there was any questions then we would get together and work it out. And do you know, there was not a single word in that contract changed? So I came back to the factory, and now we had a Les Paul model."

THE VIOLIN VAULT

Paul says that he had a much bigger involvement in the design of the Les Paul guitar than McCarty's story of the development allows. Paul states categorically: "I designed everything on there except the arched top. . . that was contributed by Maurice Berlin. Mr Berlin said to me, I like violins, and he took me by his vault and showed me his collection. And he said, We at Gibson have something that nobody else has got, a shaper so we can make a belly on that guitar. It's going to be very expensive for Fender or whoever to make one like it. He says, Would you have any objection to a violin top? And I said, It's a wonderful idea. So then they introduced me to Ted McCarty, and we signed the agreement with Gibson."

But McCarty is adamant. "I have told you exactly how it got to be a Les Paul. We spent a year designing that guitar, and Les never saw it until I took it to Pennsylvania."

Looking at photographs of Les Paul playing Gibson Les Paul guitars in the 1950s and later is instructive. Often they are specially made flat-topped instruments, whereas the production Les Pauls had an arched top. Paul nearly always modified his Gibsons in some way. As the diehard tinkerer later put it in the Capitol Records CD booklet: "By early '53 Gibson was shooting guitars to me all the time, and I was still cutting them up and modifying the pickups, bridges, controls and just about everything else." Paul evidently still had his own ideas about how a guitar should look, and in many respects these seem contrary to the way that the production models of the Gibson Les Paul guitar turned out.

It's interesting to note that after the deal was made between Paul and Gibson, they asked Paul to change the logo on the modified Epiphone models he was still using on-stage. "Gibson asked me if, until they made the Les Paul model for me, I would agree to play my Epiphone but put the name Gibson on it," explains Paul. "The plates that said Epiphone you could just pull off with a screwdriver. So I popped them off, and suggested to Ted McCarty that he send me some Gibson decals. We put them on the guitars so they would say Gibson, prior to the solidbody coming on the market."

Perhaps it will never be clear exactly who designed what on the original Gibson Les Paul model. What is certain is that Paul's respected playing and commercial success plus Gibson's weighty experience in manufacturing and marketing guitars made for a strong and impressive combination.

GIBSON'S SOLID GOLD

The new Les Paul guitar was launched by Gibson in 1952, probably in the spring, priced at $210 (about $20 more than Fender's Telecaster). Today this Les Paul model is nearly always called the 'gold-top' thanks to its gold-finished body face, and this is how we shall continue to refer to it here. The gold-top's solid body cleverly combined a carved maple top bonded to a mahogany base, this sandwich uniting the darker tonality of mahogany with the brighter sonic 'edge' of maple.

Paul says that the gold color of the original Les Paul model was his idea. "Gold means rich," he says, "expensive, the best, superb." Gibson had made a one-off all-gold hollowbody guitar in 1951 for Paul to present to a terminally ill patient whom he had met when making a special appearance at a hospital in Milwaukee. ("They were pushing my amplifier along on a cart with wheels – Mary would sing to the people and I played the guitar," says Paul.) This presentation guitar may have prompted the all-gold archtop electric ES295 model of 1952, and it could also have been the inspiration for the color of the first Les Paul model.

Almost all other design elements of the first Gibson Les Paul have precedents in earlier Gibson models. Its layout of two P90 single-coil pickups and four controls (a volume and tone per pickup) had been a feature of the previous year's L5CES and Super 400CES models. The general body outline and glued-in mahogany neck followed established Gibson traditions, and the 'crown'-shaped inlays on the rosewood fingerboard had first appeared on the 1950 incarnation of the ES150 model.

Several Gibson acoustics had already appeared with a scale-length of what the company refer to as 24.75in. 'Scale-length' is defined as double the distance from nut to 12th fret; 'string-length' is the distance from nut to bridge saddle. Gibson seem to have confused these two measurements from around 1950, and when after that time they refer in their literature to a 24.75in scale-length, they really mean string-length. As a result, the scale-length of the first and most subsequent Les Paul models is actually closer to 24.6in.

Unlike the prototype, the production model came with a new height-adjustable combined bridge/tailpiece. This was bar-shaped, and joined to it were long metal rods anchoring it to the bottom edge of the guitar. This unit was a Les Paul design, and was originally intended for use on archtop guitars; Gibson also sold it as a separate replacement accessory.

The earliest gold-tops had a very shallow neck pitch – that is to say, the neck joined the body at a rather gentle angle. This precluded use of existing Gibson hardware, and so the new bridge/tailpiece was chosen as the only suitable item.

The incorrect, overly shallow neck pitch meant that the strings were almost flat on to the body as they came off the neck. Even at its lowest setting the bridge provided a string action that was too high, so Gibson had no choice but to adapt the bridge and wrap the strings around *underneath* it. This was contrary to the intended use of the unit, designed to have the strings feeding over the top – as on the archtop, hollowbody electric Gibsons using it, such as the ES295 (1952) and the later ES225 (1955).

This set-up on the first Les Paul gold-top meant that

17

Humbucker label late 1950s
(right)
A packaging label emphasizes the
power and clarity of Gibson's new
humbucking pickups of 1957.

Seth Lover (right)
The inventor of Gibson's humbucking
pickup is pictured in the electronics
department in a 1950s catalog. Lover
had already designed for Gibson the
pickup later nicknamed the 'alnico'.

18

Gold-top 1957 (below)
In 1955 the gold-top gained Gibson's new Tune-o-matic bridge. The unit had the facility to adjust individual string-length, improving intonation. Two years later humbucking pickups replaced P90s on the gold-top, resulting in the layout seen on this refinished example.

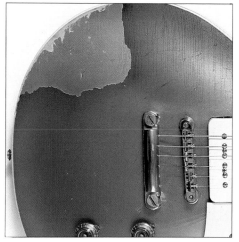

Gibson catalog 1950s (right)
Gibson were quick to exploit the name of their famous endorsee in many ways, as shown in this accessories brochure. Here is a retailer's counter display for picks, "personally selected and tested by Les Paul".

GIBSON PICK A5

LES PAUL PICKS
Personally selected and tested by Les Paul and each stamped with his name, the Les Paul picks are available in bulk lots or mounted on attractive yellow and black display cards. Card of Les Paul picks (two dozen) $2.00 each; in bulk lots for refills or individual sales $11.00 per gross or $1.00 per dozen. Specify light, medium or assorted gauges.

Gold-top 1956 close-up (left)
The third gold-top type has P90 pickups and a Tune-o-matic bridge. Note on this one the patch of wear from sweat from a player's arm, revealing the still bright gold paint under the green-ish lacquer.

19

Custom 1960 (above)
As soon as their new humbucking pickup was available Gibson changed the style of the Les Paul Custom. From 1957 the previous two-pickup layout was dropped and the guitar appeared most often with three humbuckers. This arrangement survived the change to the SG shape, but when the Custom re-appeared in 1968 its normal layout reverted to twin humbuckers.

THE SESSION MEN

No. 1 JIMMY PAGE

Jimmy Page (left)
A pre-Yardbirds Page is pictured in a 1965 magazine profile with a three-humbucker Les Paul Custom, which he'd traded for a Gretsch. In 1965 Page did up to 10 sessions a week, including work with Van Morrison's Them ('Baby Please Don't Go' and 'Here Comes The Night') and various others.

sustain suffered, intonation was inaccurate and hand-damping techniques were virtually impossible. It was clearly unworkable, as Les Paul pointed out to them. "They made the first guitar wrong," he remembers, "I don't know how many went out wrong that weren't playable. When they sent me mine, I stopped them, said this won't even play. They ran the strings under the bridge instead of over, didn't pitch the neck – they had it all screwed up."

So Gibson quickly dropped the original unit in favour of a new purpose-built bar-shaped bridge/tailpiece, mounted on the top of the body via twin height-adjustable studs. This more stable unit, with the strings now wrapped over the top of the bridge, provided improved sustain and intonation. Also, the neck pitch was steepened. The result was a much happier and more playable instrument, phased in around 1953.

Black Tuxedo, Flying Hands

The original gold-top sold well at first in relation to Gibson's other models, and in a move designed to widen the market still further for solidbody guitars Gibson issued two further Les Paul models in 1954, the Custom and the Junior. As Ted McCarty puts it: "You have all kinds of players out there who like this and like that. Chevrolet had a whole bunch of models, Ford had a whole bunch of models. . . so did we."

The two-pickup Custom looked classy with its all-black finish, multiple binding, block-shaped position markers in an ebony fingerboard, and gold-plated hardware, and was indeed pricier than the gold-top. Paul says that he chose the black color for the Custom: "Because when you're on stage with a black tuxedo and a black guitar, the people can see your hands move, with a spot on them: they'll see your hands flying." The cheaper Junior was designed for and aimed at beginners – it had a single pickup and lacked the carved top. It came finished in traditional Gibson sunburst. The September 1954 pricelist shows the Les Paul Custom at $325 and the Les Paul Junior at $99.50; the gold-top had sneaked up to $225.

The Custom had an all-mahogany body, as favored by Les Paul himself, rather than the maple/mahogany mix of the gold-top model, giving the new guitar a rather mellower tone. Paul insists that Gibson got the timber arrangements the wrong way around, and that as far as he was concerned the cheaper gold-top should have been all-mahogany, while the costlier Custom should have sported the more elaborate maple-and-mahogany combination. The Les Paul Custom was promoted in Gibson catalogues as 'The Fretless Wonder' thanks to its use of very low, flat fretwire, different to the wire used on other Les Pauls at the time.

Rectangular Reasoning

In addition to its conventional P90 at the bridge, the Custom featured a new style of pickup at the neck. This unit was soon nicknamed the 'alnico', a reference to the aluminium-nickel-cobalt alloy used for the distinctive rectangular magnetic polepieces (although alnico is certainly not unique to this pickup). It was designed by Seth Lover, a radio and electronics expert who had worked on and off for Gibson in the 1940s and early 1950s, interspersed with teaching and installation jobs for the US Navy. After several to-ings and fro-ings, Lover rejoined Gibson's electronics department permanently in 1952.

Lover had been asked to come up with a pickup that would be louder than Gibson's own P90, and louder than the single-coil Dynasonic pickup used by Gretsch (a New York-based guitar maker and a competitor to Gibson). Gretsch's unit was supplied by DeArmond, a pickup manufacturer in Toledo, Ohio.

The reason for the rectangular polepieces of the new Gibson pickup was simple, remembers Lover. "I wanted to be different, I didn't want them to be round like DeArmond's. I don't like to copy things. If you're going to improve something, make it different," he emphasizes. "Also, by making them that shape I could put screws between for height adjustment. But that pickup was never too popular because the players would always adjust them up too tight to the strings. . . they'd get that slurring type tone and they didn't like that."

The Custom was also the first Les Paul model to

receive Gibson's new Tune-o-matic bridge, used with a separate bar-shaped tailpiece. Designed by Ted McCarty, the Tune-o-matic offered for the first time on Gibsons the opportunity to adjust individually the length of each string, thus improving tuning accuracy. From 1955, it also became a feature of the gold-top model.

Although the outline of the Junior's body remained the same, the most obvious difference to its Les Paul partners was the Junior's flat-topped 'slab' mahogany body. It did not pretend to be anything other than a cheaper guitar: it had a single P90 pickup, governed by a volume and tone control, and the unbound rosewood fingerboard bore simple dot-shaped position markers. It had the wrap-over bar-shaped bridge/tailpiece as used on the second incarnation of the gold-top.

In 1955 Gibson launched the Les Paul TV model, essentially a Junior in what Gibson referred to as 'natural finish' (actually more of a yellow-ish beige color). A theory that the TV name refers to the pale color's visual prominence on monochrome television seems unfounded, as does a suggestion that 'TV' might be a less than oblique reference to the competing blond-colored Fender Telecaster. It seems more likely that the name may have been coined to cash in on Paul's regular appearances at the time on the TV show, *Les Paul & Mary Ford at Home*.

Also in 1955, the original range of Les Paul models was completed with the addition of the Special, effectively a two-pickup version of the Junior, but finished in the TV's beige color (but *not* called a TV model – a cause of much confusion since). The Special appeared on the company's September 1955 pricelist at $182.50.

Gibson added a Junior $^3/_4$ model in 1956. It had a shorter neck, giving the model a scale-length some two inches less than the normal Junior. Gibson explained in their brochure at the time that the Junior $^3/_4$ was designed to appeal to "youngsters, or adults with small hands and fingers".

Meanwhile in the Gibson electronics department, run by Walt Fuller, the industrious Seth Lover started work on another new pickup. This one would turn out to have a far greater and lasting impact than his previous design. The idea was to try to find a way to cut down the hum and electrical interference that plagued standard single-coil pickups, Gibson's ubiquitous P90 included. Lover contemplated the humbucking 'choke coil' found in some Gibson amplifiers, installed to eliminate the hum dispensed by their power transformers.

BUCKING THE HUM

"I thought," recalls Lover, "that if we can make humbucking chokes, why can't we make humbucking pickups?" No reason at all, he concluded, and started to build prototypes. The ability of such devices to buck or cut hum provides their 'humbucking' name, and the design principle is reasonably straightforward. A humbucking pickup employs two coils wired together out of phase and with opposite magnetic polarities. The result is a pickup that is less prone to picking up extraneous noise, and which gives a fatter, thicker tone than single-coil types. Additional screening is provided by a metal cover, as Lover explains.

"The cover helps shield away electrostatic noises from florescent lamps and so forth. I needed a material with high resistance, so it didn't affect the high frequency response, and I considered non-magnetic stainless steel – but you can't solder to it. German silver [an alloy of copper, nickel and zinc] has high resistance, and you could solder to it, so I used that. The prototype didn't have adjusting screws, but our sales people wanted them – so that they would have something to talk to the dealers about. So screws were added before we went into production. And for a two-pickup guitar I set the pickups in the guitars with the screws towards the bridge on the pickup nearest the bridge, and towards the fingerboard on the other. Want to know why I did that?" He laughs, and answers his own question: "For decorative purposes."

Gibson humbuckers replaced the P90 single-coil types on the Les Paul gold-top and Custom during 1957. Indeed the Custom was promoted to a three-pickup guitar in its new humbucker-equipped guise. Players gradually came to appreciate that humbuckers and a Les Paul guitar made for a congenial mixture, and today

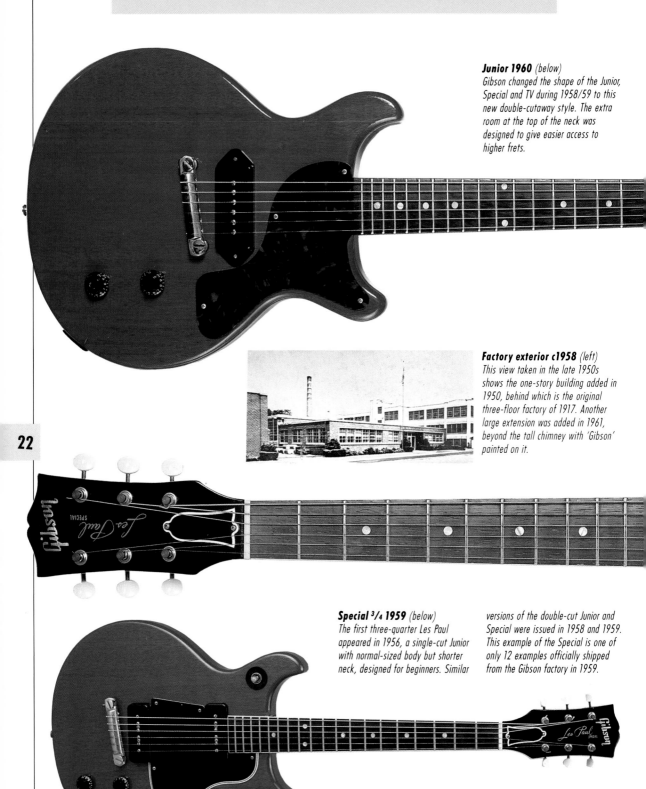

Junior 1960 (below)
Gibson changed the shape of the Junior, Special and TV during 1958/59 to this new double-cutaway style. The extra room at the top of the neck was designed to give easier access to higher frets.

Factory exterior c1958 (left)
This view taken in the late 1950s shows the one-story building added in 1950, behind which is the original three-floor factory of 1917. Another large extension was added in 1961, beyond the tall chimney with 'Gibson' painted on it.

22

Special ³/₄ 1959 (below)
The first three-quarter Les Paul appeared in 1956, a single-cut Junior with normal-sized body but shorter neck, designed for beginners. Similar versions of the double-cut Junior and Special were issued in 1958 and 1959. This example of the Special is one of only 12 examples officially shipped from the Gibson factory in 1959.

Special close-up (left)
Compare the relative positions of pickup and fingerboard on this later Special with those on the 1959 lefty (below). The proximity of the pickup to neck on early 1959 Specials (below) makes for a weak neck/body joint, often the site of breakages. Gibson quickly modified the design, moving the pickup further into the body (left) and disposing of the potential trouble-spot. (The pickguard is not original on this example.)

23

Special 1959 (above)
The double-cut Les Paul Special came and went in the same year. The change from the earlier single-cut style occurred early in 1959, while toward the end of the year Gibson removed the model's Les Paul logo, changing its name to SG Special even though everything else stayed the same. Of the 1,821 Specials shipped in 1959 only a small number would have been left-handed like this rare example.

many guitarists and collectors covet the earliest type of Gibson humbucking pickup. This is known as a 'PAF' because of the small 'patent applied for' label attached to the underside.

PATENT APPLIED FOR

Lover was not the first to come up with the idea of humbucking pickups, as he discovered when he came to patent the design (as assignor to Gibson). The patent office made reference to no fewer than six previous patents, the earliest dating from 1936. "I had a hell of a time getting a patent," Lover remembers, "and I finally got one with more or less one claim: that I'd built a humbucking pickup!" His patent application had been filed in June 1955, and was eventually issued in July 1959. Which explains the PAF label. Or does it? The PAF labels appear on pickups on guitars dated up to 1962 – well after the patent was issued. Lover has a theory to explain this: "Gibson didn't want to give any information as to what patent to look up for those who wanted to make copies. I think that was the reason they carried on with the PAF label for quite a while." When they eventually got around to putting a patent number on the pickup, Gibson also deterred budding copyists by 'mistakenly' making it the number for a bridge patent.

Players who say that they prefer the sound of PAF-label humbuckers cite the apparently negative sonic differences of later versions caused by small changes to coil-winding, magnet grades and wire-sheathing. Today, Seth Lover cannot recall any alterations made to his invention during the transition from those with PAF label to the later units stamped with patent numbers. "The only change that I'm aware of is that from time to time Gibson would use gold plating on the covers, and I think if they got the gold plating a little heavy then the pickups would tend to lose the high frequencies, because gold is a very good conductor."

The July 1957 pricelist details the Les Paul line-up as follows: Les Paul Custom (black) $375; Les Paul gold-top $247.50; Les Paul Special (beige) $179.50; Les Paul TV (beige) $132.50; Les Paul Junior (sunburst) $120; Les Paul Junior 3/4 (sunburst) $120. Gibson's sales of these

original Les Paul guitars in general hit a peak in 1956 and 1957, and it is upon these models that most of Gibson's later theme-and-variation of Les Paul designs would be based. A number of well-known players from a variety of musical styles were drawn to Gibson Les Pauls in the 1950s, including Frannie Beecher from Bill Haley and the Comets, bluesmen like Guitar Slim, Freddie King and John Lee Hooker, rockabilly rebel Carl Perkins, and many more.

DOUBLE-CUT CHERRIES

In 1958 Gibson made a radical design change to three of the Les Paul models, and a cosmetic alteration to another. The Junior, Junior 3/4 and TV were revamped with a completely new double-cutaway body shape. Ted McCarty explains the re-design as a reaction to player's requests. "They wanted to be able to thumb the sixth string, and they couldn't do it if the only cutaway was over on the treble side. So we made them with another cutaway, so they could get up there. We did things that the players wanted, as much as anything." The Junior's fresh look was enhanced with a new cherry red finish. The TV adopted the new double-cutaway design as well, along with a rather more yellow-ish color.

When the double-cutaway design was applied to the Special in the following year, the result was not an immediate success. Gibson overlooked the fact that the cavity for the neck pickup in the Special's new body severely weakened the neck/body joint, and many a neck was snapped right off at this point. The error was soon corrected by moving the neck pickup further down the body, resulting in a stronger joint. The new double-cutaway Special was offered in cherry or the new TV yellow (although, again causing much confusion later, the yellow Special was never actually called a TV model).

Sales of the Les Paul gold-top model in particular had begun to decline, so in 1958 Gibson changed its look by applying their more traditional cherry sunburst finish, in a bid to sell more guitars. Despite the wide use later among players and collectors of the name 'Standard' for this sunburst model, Gibson did not refer to it as the Les Paul Standard in their literature until 1960, and the guitar never bore the name. We shall generally refer to this model as the Sunburst.

A Gibson employee explains the change to sunburst finish in this way: "Something had to be done to stimulate more interest. So those few years of the Sunburst model were basically planned to help regenerate increased interest in the Les Paul." Even though production was higher in 1959 and 1960 than in the previous two years, the increase was still only a modest one, and the Sunburst model was dropped during 1960.

Indeed the Sunburst Gibson Les Paul, or 'burst' in guitar-buff parlance, was made only between 1958 and 1960, and Gibson's November 1959 pricelist shows it at $280. Among players and collectors it has since become the most highly prized solidbody electric guitar ever. 'Bursts' regularly fetch huge sums, far in excess of other collectable solids, and the factor which above all determines the magnitude of their value is not usually related to the sound or playability of the guitars at all, but to their look.

Gold-top models often had maple tops made from two or more pieces of wood, safely hidden under the gold paint. Now that this maple top was on show through the transparent sunburst finish, Gibson's woodworkers were more careful with its appearance, and would usually bookmatch the timber. Bookmatching is a technique where a piece of wood is split into two, then opened out down a central join (like a book) to give symmetrically matching grain patterns.

BURSTING INTO FLAMES

The most celebrated 'bursts' are those with the most outrageous wood patterns visible through the top's finish. The woodworker's term for these patterns on timber is 'figure', and while any tree can potentially produce figured timber, the means by which it occurs is nevertheless an unpredictable fluke. Some trees will have it, some will not.

Figure is caused by a kind of genetic anomaly in the growing tree that makes ripples in the cells of the living wood. The visual effect of figure is also determined by

color variations in the tree's growth, the effect of disease or damage, and the way in which the timber is cut from the felled tree. Quarter-sawing – that is cutting so that the grain is generally square to the face of the resulting planks – often produces the most attractive results with the illusion of roughly parallel rows of three-dimensional 'fingers' or 'hills and valleys' going across the face of the timber. In extreme cases this can look spectacular.

Such cosmetics are accorded many descriptive terms, including 'fiddleback' or 'tigerstripe', but the most common seems to be 'flamed'. Although technically this refers to a different effect, the term has taken hold among dealers, players and collectors, and now has to be considered correct.

FADING FAST

The eventual visual quality of the 1958-60 Les Paul Sunburst models was, therefore, a hit-and-miss affair purely based on the timber that came out of Gibson's store during that period. It seems that the company's most impressively figured maple was used for the backs of their archtop guitars, but even so some Les Paul Sunbursts are astonishingly attractive. And, by the same token, some are extremely plain.

There is another factor that can also make Sunburst models look markedly different from one another. The colored paints used to create the sunburst effect, especially the red element, can fade in varying ways, depending primarily on how the guitar has been exposed to daylight during its lifetime. Some apparently sharp-eyed collectors claim to be able to tell how long a particular guitar spent in the shop window. In some cases the original shaded sunbursting can have almost totally disappeared, leaving the guitar with a uniform and rather pleasing honey color.

Those who do get the chance to play these guitars rather than consign them to bank-vaults as part of an investment portfolio have noted a number of minor changes over the three years of production: small frets in 1958, bigger during 1959-60; a chunky, round-backed neck over the 1958-59 period, and a slimmer, flatter-profiled version in 1960. But as one US guitar dealer puts

Sunburst 1958: Jimmy Page's No.1 (below)

This is Page's first-choice stage and studio guitar, and the wear and tear of innumerable tours and sessions have taken their toll. Unlike some guitars of this vintage, Page's 'No.1' is quite clearly for playing: this is the one he likes best. The guitar is thought to be from 1958, although it lost its serial number during headstock repairs some time ago, and the non-original bridge pickup has long been without its cover, revealing twin black bobbins.

Binding differences (left)

The view inside a Les Paul's cutaway can sometimes give clues to the guitar's age. Examples from the 1950s generally have a strip of binding (far left) following the contour of the body top (as have some re-issues). Normal-issue Les Pauls since the late 1960s tend to have a deeper strip of binding (left) with a straight edge following the maple/mahogany join.

26

Sunburst 1992: Jimmy Page's No.3 *(above)*
This is a duplicate of No.1, made for Page by Roger Giffin of Gibson's West Coast Custom Shop as a backup for the 1958 Sunburst. The rear of the headstock (not shown) has 'J PAGE' stamped in the position where one would normally expect to see a serial number on ordinary production Les Pauls.

27

Sunburst 1959: Jimmy Page's No.2 *(above)*
This instrument was a gift from Joe Walsh and, like No.1, is a worn and faded Sunburst. To improve the sound but preserve the guitar it has had two black pushbuttons added under the pickguard (just visible in our picture) for phase and series/parallel switching with both pickups on, while the control pots are push/pull types offering coil-taps and series/parallel for individual pickups. (As with No. 1, the original tuners have been replaced.)

Eric Clapton *(left)*
Clapton did most to popularize Les Pauls during the late 1960s, in John Mayall's Bluesbreakers, and Cream. This shot is from a 1967 Beat Instrumental; note the Sunburst with pickguard removed. "You've probably heard about me taking the covers off my pickups. The improvement soundwise is unbelievable," he claimed.

it: "It seems like the top more than anything else will sell those guitars. If it has a killer top but it's beat to hell and refinished it'll still sell for more than one that's plain. The high prices are due I think to the fact that non-players are paying the most money for them, and these people go solely for the look. I've seen them buy those guitars without even plugging them in. And they've missed some great guitars because they've looked and said, Nah, not interested, no top. . . "

LOOKING FOR ZEBRAS

There is one more feature from this period that seems to belong more to collecting stamps than guitars. In the very late 1950s Hughes Plastics, one of Gibson's suppliers of plastic components, ran out of black plastic for the pickup 'bobbin', the former around which the pickup wire is wound. Cream plastic was substituted for a while, and years later a fashion for removing pickup covers revealed the different colors. Some over-excited collectors and players even began to pay more for guitars with all-cream or cream-and-black bobbins (the latter known as 'zebra' pickups among burst obsessives).

Humbucker inventor Seth Lover illuminates the picture: "Yes, our supplier ran out of black material, but they did have cream. We were not going to stop production just for that," he laughs, "so we got some cream bobbins. I couldn't tell any difference one from the other. . . although I think cream was a better color for winding because you could see the wire in there a lot easier than you could with the black."

Considering all the Les Paul models as a whole, sales declined in 1960 after a peak in 1959. By 1961 Gibson had decided on a complete re-design of the line in an effort to try to reactivate this faltering market.

Gibson had started a $400,000 expansion of their factory in Kalamazoo during 1960 which more than doubled the size of the plant by the time it was completed in 1961. It was the third addition to the original 1917 factory, other buildings having been added in 1945 and 1950. But this new single story brick-and-steel building was more than twice the size of previous additions combined, resulting in a plant of more than

120,000 square feet that extended for two city blocks at Parsons Street in Kalamazoo.

One of the first series of new models to benefit from Gibson's newly expanded production facilities was the completely revised Les Paul design. Before we recount the stories concerning the new guitars, it's worth clearing up the confusion concerning the variety of names allocated by Gibson to the Les Paul models and designs from 1959 to 1963. This is what happened:

(1) The new model name of SG, standing for 'solid guitar', was first given to a Gibson instrument in 1959. The design style of the double-cutaway Les Paul TV continued, but late in 1959 it was issued without the 'Les Paul TV' logo applied to its headstock, and became the SG TV model. The same thing happened to the Les Paul Special and the Les Paul Special $^3/_4$ models, which in late 1959 became the SG Special and the SG Special $^3/_4$. Gibson's sales literature, as usual behind such changes, used the new SG TV name by 1960 and the new SG Special and SG Special $^3/_4$ names by 1961.

(2) The Les Paul Junior $^3/_4$ was dropped in 1961.

(3) The Les Paul Junior, 'Standard' and Custom were completely re-designed in 1961. The familiar single-cutaway body style was dropped, and the new instruments featured a radical double-cutaway body with highly sculpted edges. Juniors and Customs from 1961 can be of either shape, but 'Standards' (Sunbursts) of the old style stopped in 1960. Initially, Gibson retained the Les Paul name on the re-designed versions: on the headstock of the Junior, on the truss-rod cover of the Standard, and on a plate on the body of the Custom.

(4) During 1963 Gibson dropped the Les Paul name from the re-designed Les Paul Junior, Les Paul Standard and Les Paul Custom, and in their literature gradually re-named these instruments as the SG Junior, the SG Standard and the SG Custom.

(5) In retrospect, the re-designed Juniors, Standards and Customs referred to in (3) above are today generally referred to by players and collectors as 'SG/Les Paul' models. 'SG' relates to the later official name of the body shape, 'Les Paul' to the logo retained on the models made from 1961 to 1963.

There are a number of different stories concerning the eventual removal of Les Paul's name from the newly-designed Gibson 'SG/Les Paul' models in 1963. Ted McCarty, still president of Gibson, says that it was done because of various factors which made the association with Paul less of a commercial bonus than it had been.

The popularity of Les Paul as a recording artist had declined: Les Paul & Mary Ford had no more Top 40 hits on Capitol after 1955, and left the label in 1958. They joined Columbia for a few years, but with little success.

Paul and Ford's personal relationship was apparently deteriorating. Their separation was reported in the recording trade magazine *Billboard* in May 1963: "Miss Ford is now living in California, while Paul is living in New Jersey," ran the news item on the bottom of an inside page, under the headline: "Les and Mary Say Bye-Bye." The couple were officially divorced by the end of 1964, and Paul retired from most playing and recording for about ten years from 1965.

NAME-DROPPING

The main reason why Les Paul's name was dropped from Gibson guitars in 1963 relates to the divorce of Paul and Ford. "The contract came due I think in 1962," recalls Paul, "right at the time that Mary and I decided to split." He and Gibson agreed, he says, that they would wait until the divorce was over before further discussions. Paul did not want to sign any fresh contract bringing in new money while the divorce proceedings were underway, he says, "because [Ford's] lawyers would ask for part of it in the divorce settlement. So my contract ended in '62 and Gibson could not make any more Les Paul guitars."

Paul also says that he didn't like the design of the new SG/Les Paul models, and that this was an additional reason for the removal of his name from them. It's this reason which has most often been given prominence. In 1978, for example, Paul told Tom Wheeler in *American Guitars*: "The first [SG/Les Paul] I saw was in a music store... and I didn't like the shape – a guy could kill himself on those sharp horns. It was too thin, and they had moved the front pickup away from the fingerboard so they could fit my name in there. The neck was too

skinny and I didn't like the way it joined the body; there wasn't enough wood, at least in my opinion. So I called Gibson and asked them to take my name off the thing. It wasn't my design."

Nonetheless, Paul is seen in various official Gibson promotional photographs with the SG/Les Paul models, and holds one on the cover of his album "Les Paul Now".

ULTRA THIN, HAND CONTOURED

The American musical instrument business magazine *Music Trades* from August 1961 carries a report of the gala banquet given at the close of the July NAMM trade show (the National Association of Music Merchants). Star turn at the banquet was Les Paul & Mary Ford, and the photo in the magazine report clearly shows both Paul and Ford playing old-style single-cutaway Gibson Les Pauls. Elsewhere in the same issue is a Gibson advertisement headed 'Solid Hit' with a drawing of Paul and Ford, promoting the new SG/Les Paul models ("ultra thin, hand contoured, double cutaway"). So Paul, still under his Gibson contract, continued to play the original style of Gibson Les Paul on stage, but at the same time Gibson used him to push the new SG-style guitars.

Production of Les Paul models did increase slightly when the new SG-style designs were introduced during 1961, with output of Gibson Les Pauls from Kalamazoo settling at just under 6000 units per year for 1961, 1962 and 1963. Gibson's pricelist of September 1963 is among the last in the early 1960s to feature Les Pauls, and itemises three models: the 'SG/Les Paul' Custom (white) at $450; 'SG/Les Paul' Standard (cherry) at $310; and 'SG/Les Paul' Junior (cherry) at $155.

From 1964 until 1967 inclusive there were no guitars in the Gibson line bearing the Les Paul name, either on the guitars themselves or in the company's literature.

SALES & STRIKES

Guitar sales in general in the United States – including acoustic as well as electric instruments – climbed throughout the early 1960s, and hit a peak of some 1,500,000 units in 1965, after which sales declined and fell to just over a million in 1967. CMI's sales of Gibson

Sunburst 1959: Peter Green/ Gary Moore (above)
Around 1970 Gary Moore acquired this guitar from Peter Green, who probably used it on most early Fleetwood Mac tracks. Moore has played it extensively since. Damage to the headstock suffered by the guitar in a car crash is visible. The neck pickup was already reversed when Moore got the guitar, but has never been 'corrected' for fear of spoiling the guitar's distinctive sounds.

30

Jeff Beck's Third Les Paul (above)
Pickup specialist Seymour Duncan acquired this guitar for Beck; it's the one he used on "Blow By Blow" (see opposite page). Despite the black look of the non-original finish, it is in fact a very dark brown.

Peter Green *(right)*
The 20 year-old is seen here in a 1966 profile announcing his employment by John Mayall as replacement for the outgoing Eric Clapton. Green explained that stepping into Clapton's shoes made him try too hard and overplay sometimes: "If I make a mistake I'm spoiled for the rest of the evening." The Sunburst is possibly that pictured left, now owned and played by Gary Moore.

31

Jeff Beck's Second Les Paul *(above)*
This was Beck's second Sunburst, which he stripped down to the wood in 1968 to resemble a pale Les Paul he admired in a Gibson catalog. He used this guitar in The Jeff Beck Group (1967-72) and on singles like 'Hi Ho Silver Lining' and

'Barabajagal'. A repairer in Memphis later replaced the original pickups, thinned the neck, added 'JB' at the 22nd fret, and inlaid an old-style Gibson logo and 'flower-pot' motif into the headstock. Beck was not amused; he describes the result as "revolting".

Jeff Beck "Blow By Blow" *(right)*
The rear of the sleeve of this notable album, released in 1975, shows Beck playing the brown Les Paul pictured left. This was his main guitar for the recording, produced by George Martin, although there's also a humbuckered Fender Telecaster in evidence. Beck also started to use a Fender Stratocaster on some of the tracks, and it is with this make and model of guitar that he has been most closely associated ever since.

guitars and amplifiers hit a peak of $19 million in 1966, but then began to fall in line with the general trend, down to $15 million by 1968.

As well as the general decline in demand for guitars, Gibson's production had been hit by a number of strikes in the 1960s, including a 16-day stoppage in 1966 which, said *Music Trades*, resulted in a "turnover of skilled personnel" and meant that "production efficiency at Gibson remained at relatively low levels throughout the year". Gibson was also not helped by adverse local weather conditions, nor when "a trucking industry strike in the Chicago area interrupted the flow of merchandise in and out of the company's distribution center".

A new home for Gibson's electronics department had been built in 1962, and a separate factory intended for the manufacturing of Gibson amplification, strings and pickups was purchased in 1964. Guitar manufacturing remained at Parsons Street, Kalamazoo. Gibson president Ted McCarty and his number two, John Huis, left in 1966 after purchasing the Bigsby musical accessories company of California, which they re-established in Kalamazoo.

In February 1968, after a number of short-stay occupants in the president's chair, Stan Rendell was appointed president of Gibson. Rendell had worked for CMI since 1963 and was vice president of manufacturing. He told his boss, Maurice Berlin, that he was tired of travelling so much between the plants associated with CMI's various products, which included Lowrey organs and Olds brass as well as Gibson. Berlin offered Rendell the chance to run Gibson – a challenge, as it turned out. "Mr Berlin said to me, You know, we're not doing too well with Gibson," remembers Rendell. "They had lost a million dollars at the factory for the two prior years." So Rendell was made president of Gibson, and set about his assignment of improving the company's fortunes.

Guitarist Bruce Bolen was born in England and raised in Chicago. He was employed by Gibson in 1967 to organise and perform promotional shows and concerts for the company and, as Bolen describes it, "to be a representative player for Gibson". Gradually over the years Bolen took on more responsibility, eventually becoming involved in guitar design and marketing.

Back in the late 1960s when he joined the company, Bolen too remembers the poor state of Gibson operations. "One of the reasons I was hired was because Gibson's electric sales were floundering. All we had in solid electrics were SGs, plus the arched-top and thinline instruments, and they weren't selling all that well. The mainstay of the company at the time was the flat-top acoustics. So I was hired basically to go out and sell electric guitars."

He found that the management at CMI and Gibson were generally unaware during the late 1960s of the growing interest among rock guitarists in the original Les Paul models. "I was just a punk kid, and most of the people there were in their 50s or older," Bolen recalls. "I don't think they had a great grasp on how important that guitar was becoming once again. The Mike Bloomfields, Eric Claptons, they'd found it to be something really precious that offered a sound that was very conducive to their form of music."

BLOOMFIELD IN THE USA

From around 1965 there was a boom in blues-based rock music. Many white guitarists were at the core of this new musical movement, some inspired by the guitars used by their black influences. They discovered that a Gibson Les Paul overdriven through powerful valve amplifiers and multiple loudspeaker cabinets produced a wonderfully rich, emotive sound that was well suited to this fresh musical setting.

Michael Bloomfield in the United States had first come to general attention when he donned a Fender Telecaster to play electric guitar behind Bob Dylan at the singer's infamous first all-electric concert at the 1965 Newport Folk Festival. Bloomfield went on to appear on Dylan's 'Highway 61 Revisited' album in the same year. Shortly afterwards he picked up his first Les Paul, a gold-top, and soon acquired a Sunburst. This he used while a permanent member of the Butterfield Blues Band on their improvisational 'East-West' LP in 1966, its strong flavors of Indian music and jazz hitting a popular chord at the time.

Bloomfield's 'Super Session' album of 1968 with Steve

Stills and Al Kooper was a platinum best-seller. His appearance on the cover of that record with a Les Paul Sunburst did much to promote the guitar's growing popularity among guitarists in America. Tragically in 1981 Mike Bloomfield died from drug-related causes, aged 36.

CLAPTON IN THE UK

In the UK the most notable member of the Les Paul guitar appreciation society was Eric Clapton. "The best Les Paul I ever had was stolen during rehearsals for Cream's first gig," he told *Guitar Player*, the respected US magazine for guitarists, in July 1985. "It was the one I had with John Mayall – just a regular sunburst Les Paul that I bought in one of the shops in London right after I'd seen Freddie King's album cover of 'Let's Hide Away and Dance Away,' where he's playing a gold-top. It had humbuckers and was almost brand new – original case with that lovely purple velvet lining, just magnificent. I never really found one as good as that. I do miss that one." Incidentally, this loss has given rise today among a number of hopeful Sunburst owners to unsubstantiated claims that their Les Paul is the 'ex-Bluesbreakers' guitar.

As a member of John Mayall's Bluesbreakers, Clapton played a Les Paul Sunburst to great effect on the group's 'Blues Breakers' LP. This famous 'Beano-cover' album came out in July 1966, a month before the Butterfield Blues Band's 'East-West' was released featuring Bloomfield's playing. Despite the timing of record releases, it was Bloomfield in America and Clapton in Britain who, more than any other musicians, were turning fellow players' ears toward the new sound of the old Les Paul guitars.

In Britain the search for old Les Pauls grew ever more urgent as a queue of respected players formed to take up the aging model. Keith Richards of the Rolling Stones had been among the first star guitarists to be seen with a Gibson Les Paul after bringing back a Sunburst model from the group's June 1964 US tour. Jimmy Page used a triple-pickup Custom when he was a busy session player on the London recording scene in the mid-1960s, and went on to play Sunbursts at the end of the 1960s with Led Zeppelin. Jeff Beck was inspired to move from a Fender Esquire to a Les Paul Sunburst after seeing Eric Clapton play one with Mayall's Bluesbreakers in London. Clapton's replacement in Mayall's band, Peter Green, used a Sunburst to great effect in that group and also in Fleetwood Mac which he formed in 1967.

Prices for secondhand instruments began gradually to climb, and letters pleading for help in locating these elusive old Les Pauls appeared in the musicians' press. "I am having great difficulty in obtaining a Gibson Les Paul Custom guitar," wrote an A P Jones of Essex in the August 1967 issue of *Beat Instrumental*, the top monthly magazine for rock musicians in Britain at the time. "Have you any idea where I can obtain one? If you think this is impossible, perhaps you could tell me which guitar is similar in tone?"

While the query specified the Custom, most guitarists would have been pleased to find any guitar with the Les Paul name on it. The magazine replied: "The Les Paul Custom is a much sought after instrument. It is impossible to obtain a new one, and even secondhand models are very scarce. If you want one, then you will have to be very patient." *Beat* went on to recommend as an alternative one of the slowly growing band of Japanese-made copy guitars being imported to Europe and the US. These oriental 'replicas' were actually of pretty poor quality at the time, but at least they looked similar and were available.

LEGENDARY LES PAULS

The search for Les Pauls did not abate. Again, in a news item in the October issue of the same year, *Beat* contemplated the sad state of supply and demand. They wrote: "So many people are interested in obtaining one of the almost legendary Les Paul guitars that we've done a bit of checking. . . " and went on to give some spurious information concerning dates and models – excusable given the lack of general knowledge about guitar history back in 1967. *Beat* concluded: "Some guitarists insist that new Les Pauls can still be bought, but they're wrong. . . so if you're offered a guitar, and told it's a Les Paul, be very wary."

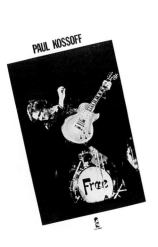

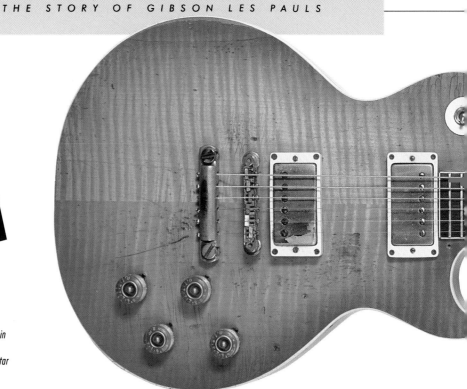

Paul Kossoff (above)
This Island Records publicity
photograph shows the Free guitarist in
the early 1970s playing a Les Paul
Sunburst, which may well be the guitar
pictured right.

34

Sunburst: ex-Paul Kossoff
(below)
During his brief career, from Free's first album (1968) to his last work with Back Street Crawler (1975), Kossoff used a number of Les Pauls. This one was sold to its present owner, Arthur Ramm, by Kossoff's family after the 25 year-old's untimely death in 1976. Guitarist Ramm had become acquainted with Kossoff while supporting Free in his band Beckett.

'Unburst' close-up *(right)*
The red element of the sunburst finish on some Les Pauls from the 1958-1960 period is prone to fade when exposed to daylight, leading in some cases to a pleasant and almost uniform honey color. Such guitars are often nicknamed 'unburst' Les Pauls. Parts of the body that remain covered, such as the area under the switch ring and, as shown here, under the pickguard, often retain traces of the original red color.

George Harrison's Les Paul
(below)
This unusual red Les Paul originally belonged to Eric Clapton, who in 1968 used it to record the solo on The Beatles' 'While My Guitar Gently Weeps', and gave it to George Harrison. "Then it got kidnapped and taken to Guadalajara," Harrison told Guitar Player. "I had to buy this Mexican guy a Les Paul to get it back." The off-center join implies that it may be a refinished gold-top.

35

The Beatles *(right)*
An EMI/Apple black-and-white publicity shot shows Harrison (second from the right) with the red Les Paul pictured above. The photo is a still from a promotional film the group made in September 1968 for 'Revolution'.

Gibson at last decided to do something about their deteriorating position in the electric guitar market, and specifically about the increasing demand for their old Les Paul guitars.

Bruce Bolen, Gibson's 'guitar-playing representative', remembers that one day soon after he started working for the company in 1967 vice president Marc Carlucci asked if he'd mind staying late that evening at the CMI headquarters in Chicago. "Marc said, We've got someone coming in and we want your opinion on what he has to show us. I said, Who is it? And he said, Les Paul.

"Now when I was a kid, six years old, Les Paul was my first guitar hero," Bolen continues, "so I was thrilled to have the chance to meet him. Gibson still wasn't too sure they wanted to reintroduce the Les Paul again. I was going: please!"

Les Paul's musical activities had been very low-key since the mid-1960s, but this meeting in 1967 marked the start of his new association with Gibson and the beginning of the re-issue programme for Les Paul models. Paul's recollection of the circumstances is typically forthright: "I called Gibson and said hey, Fender's here bugging me and they want to make a deal, and my divorce is over. I said, Do you want to make a deal? And Mr Berlin said, Odd you should call, because we're striking all electrical instruments from the Gibson line. He said, The electric guitar is extinct. And I says, Can I meet you Friday in Chicago? I want to buy you a cup of coffee. We stayed up for 24 hours, and I convinced him to go back and make the electric guitar."

Maybe Mr Berlin really was thinking about "striking all electrical instruments from the Gibson line," but there's little evidence of such a move being contemplated. Regardless, Gibson negotiated a new contract with Paul, and it seems likely that the royalty paid to him was in the region of five per cent of the 'standard cost' of each Les Paul model – that is, the internal price at which Gibson sold the guitar to CMI, which was around a third of retail. Such a calculation would, for example, result in Paul receiving about $6.50 for each Les Paul model typically selling for $395 retail.

By the time Stan Rendell became president of Gibson

in early 1968, the decision to re-commence manufacturing Les Paul guitars had been made by the CMI management in Chicago, principally by Maurice Berlin and Marc Carlucci.

At the Gibson plant in Kalamazoo, Rendell and his team had their own difficulties. Rendell recalls the position when he joined Gibson: "We had all kinds of quality problems. We had production problems. We had personnel problems. We had union problems. We had problems that wouldn't end."

Rendell, the new broom, set to work. He developed a structure to the supervision in Gibson's Kalamazoo factory, instigated manufacturing schedules, improved inspection routines, installed a separate stock room, held regular meetings, and bought, as he puts it, "a ton of new equipment, all sorts of stuff. Mr Berlin said that in the first five years I was there, there were more new ideas, new machinery and new products than in the entire history of the Gibson company prior to that. We just had a ball, we had a lot of fun. And if we didn't know how to do something, we found out."

Bruce Bolen, meanwhile, had a showstopper for his Gibson promotional concerts. He'd taken out on the road a prototype of the forthcoming Les Paul Custom, as far as he can remember by very late 1967. "People were just falling apart about it, they couldn't wait to get one."

LES PAULS: THE COMEBACK

Gibson decided to re-introduce the relatively rare two-pickup Les Paul Custom, and the gold-top Les Paul with P90 pickups and Tune-o-matic bridge. There was some initial discussion about making the Custom in white, as the SG/Les Paul Custom had been, but the sensitivity of white lacquer to contamination made the company go with the 'correct' black version.

Gibson formally launched the two new models at the June 1968 NAMM trade show in Chicago. The company's pricelist from that month shows the two revived Les Pauls for the first time: the Custom is pitched at $545 and the gold-top at $395. Throughout this period Gibson in their literature called the gold-top a 'Standard' model. This was rather confusing since they had never officially referred to the gold-top as anything but a 'Les Paul Model' or 'Les Paul Guitar' during the 1950s. For continuity, we shall carry on calling these guitars gold-tops.

Les Paul was at the NAMM show to promote the new guitars for Gibson by doing what he's always done best – playing the things. Bolen remembers: "I provided the rhythm section for Les, and it was the first time in years that he'd got on a stage. We had a lot of fun."

Gibson's press advertisement publicizing the revived guitars, headed "Daddy of 'em all," admitted that Gibson had virtually been forced to re-introduce the guitars: "The demand for them just won't quit. And the pressure to make more has never let up. Okay, you win. We are pleased to announce that more of the original Les Paul Gibsons are available. Line forms at your Gibson dealer. . . "

Soon after the summer '68 NAMM show, production of the new Customs and gold-tops was started at Kalamazoo. Rendell says that the first run, which took 90 days to get from wood shop to stock room, was for 500 guitars: 400 gold-tops and 100 Customs. "And by the time we had that started, CMI wanted 100 a month of the gold-top and 25 a month of the Custom, and before we were finished with that we were making a hundred Les Pauls a day. That's out of a total of 250, 300 instruments a day." Gibson clearly had a success in the making; the only mystery as far as many guitarists were concerned was why they'd waited so long.

CMI + ECL = NORLIN

An important change to Gibson's ownership occurred in 1969. The musical instrument business magazine *Music Trades* reported that the new owner, Norlin Industries, came into being in 1969 with the merger of CMI and ECL, an Ecuadorian brewery. ECL simply bought enough of CMI's publicly traded stock to gain control of the company. The Norlin name was arrived at by combining the first syllable of ECL chairman Norton Stevens' name with the last syllable of that of CMI founder Maurice Berlin. Norlin was in three businesses: musical instruments, brewing, and what *Music Trades*

described loosely as 'technology'. The takeover was formalized in 1974 and Maurice Berlin, a man widely respected in the musical instrument industry, was moved sideways in the new structure, away from the general running of the company.

Many people who worked for Gibson at the time have said how, when the change of ownership occurred, there was suddenly a new breed of employee to be seen. The most common description – and indeed the most polite – is of a be-suited Harvard MBA with slide-rule and calculator at the ready. In more detail, that's a Master of Business Administration graduate from the Harvard Business School, armed with the requisite tools of his trade. Or, as one Gibson manager of the time puts it: "I'd think about people, about machines, about parts. . . and these new guys'd 'solve' all the problems with a calculator. They had nothing to offer, other than that they were looking for a place to invest their money and gain a profit, that was their motivation."

Gibson president Stan Rendell remembers that the new owners made a fundamental change to the way his business operated. "When they came in, they said we're going to change Gibson from a profit center to a cost center. Before, we sold guitars to CMI, which meant that we could make a profit at the factory. And with that profit we were able to buy machinery, improve the benefits to the employees, increase the rates of pay, everything that a company that makes a profit can do. But when they changed us to a cost center we had no sales – they just paid our bills. And when they did that they destroyed the initiative. If someone runs up a bill, it's paid. So the person running up the bill doesn't have any incentive to not run it so high or not run it at all."

Many Gibson people from this period feel that there was a move away from managers who understood guitars to managers who understood manufacturing. Some of the instruments made during the period soon after Gibson were taken over have a bad reputation today. The new owners are generally felt now to have been insensitive to the needs of musicians. One insider remembers: "Up until about 1974 everything was hunky dory, and then it began to change. Too many people were

38

SG/Les Paul Standard 1961
(below)
The new 'SG' shape – with twin cutaways, sharp horns and beveled edges – was applied to the Les Paul Junior, Standard and Custom models in 1961. The example shown has Gibson's unusual sideways-action vibrato, as do many SG/Les Paul Standards and Customs. Players were meant to operate it with an in-and-out action rather than the customary up-and-down movement. The unit was not successful and did not last long.

"Les Paul Now" *(above)*
Les Paul came out of 'retirement' in the late 1960s to release this album of re-recorded instrumental versions of some of his best-known 1950s work, such as 'How High The Moon'. The sleeve shows an unusual two-pickup SG/Les Paul Custom.

Gibson ad 1961 *(right)*
A press advertisement announces the new design for the Les Paul models, and features an SG/Les Paul Custom: "Beauty in gleaming white or cherry red that must be seen," it proclaims.

SG/Les Paul Custom 1961 *(below)*
This model continued the idea that the Custom should be the most expensive guitar – and the most expensive looking guitar – in the normal Les Paul line. The restored gold hardware of this example sits handsomely against Gibson's "gleaming white" finish, and gives a good indication of how striking the guitar must have looked when new over 30 years ago.

SG/Les Paul Junior 1961 *(below)*
The second re-styling of the Junior occurred during 1961, when the rounded-horn double-cut body of 1958-61 was replaced with the sharp-horned 'SG' body. But the inherent simplicity of the Junior lived on, as did Gibson's famous cherry red finish.

Junior vibrato close-up *(left)*
While some SG/Les Paul Juniors came with the straightforward combined bridge/tailpiece as on the example below, a number were offered with this optional vibrato unit, separate from the bridge and of relatively simple design.

39

Les Paul & Mary Ford *(above)*
The musical couple pose (left) for a studio photographer with what appears to be a modified SG/Les Paul Custom with only two pickups. On the Columbia EP sleeve (right) they hold rather more conventional SG/Les Pauls: a cherry Standard, and a white Custom.

doing too few things, too much money was being spent on too little, and it started to affect the infamous bottom line."

It's interesting to note that this air of retrospective uneasiness is mirrored in the case of two other American guitar-making giants which were also taken over during the period in question: Fender (by CBS in 1965) and Gretsch (by Baldwin in 1967). Clearly this was a sign of the times, as economic analysts advised big corporations to diversify into a range of different areas, pour in some money, and sit back to wait for the profits.

At any rate, Gibson was not alone in feeling the effects that the new management methods were causing. This shift in emphasis toward the rationalisation of production meant that changes were made to some of the Gibson guitars built during the 1970s (and, to some extent, into the 1980s). Generally, such alterations were made for one of three reasons: (1) to save money; (2) to limit the number of guitars returned for work under warranty; and (3) to speed up production.

The most common remark made about Gibson Les Pauls from the 1970s is a generalisation that many of them are relatively heavy when compared to examples from other periods. This was partly due to the increase in density of the mahogany that Gibson was buying, but also to a change in body construction that lasted from about 1969 to circa 1973.

Instead of the traditional maple/mahogany combination or all-mahogany construction, an elaborate multiple sandwich was developed. This consisted of a maple top, with twin layers of mahogany underneath divided by another layer of thin maple. As one looks at the side of a Les Paul with this construction the extra central stripe of maple should be discernible.

The effect of adding an extra piece of timber in this way, with a contrary grain pattern, is known as cross-banding. Gibson's internal ECN (Engineering Change Notice) says that it was done to strengthen the body, to prevent cracking and checking. "It's a standard practice in the furniture industry," says Stan Rendell. "It ties the wood together."

It may also have simplified Norlin's timber buying,

because it meant that the thinner pieces of mahogany already used for necks could now also be utilized for bodies. But by about 1973 the cross-banding had been stopped: there were complaints about shrinkage around the obvious joins, and the extra labour costs involved in preparing the sandwich priced it out of contention.

Gibson changed their neck construction around 1969, moving from traditional one-piece mahogany to a stronger three-piece laminate, and on to three-piece maple around 1974 for even greater strength. From about 1969 they added a so-called 'volute' to the back of the neck just below the point where it becomes the headstock – a sort of triangular 'lump' that theoretically reinforces this notoriously weak spot. Another change made to minimize problems in the same area was introduced at this time, when Gibson slightly decreased the angle at which the headstock tipped back from the neck. Such seemingly practical changes did nothing to enhance Gibson's reputation among traditionalists.

EPI HUNTING GROUND

Also courtesy of the busy guitar design department at Gibson, the recently re-introduced gold-top model was given a change of style and name. Effectively, this meant that the first revitalized gold-top lasted for only a short time, from 1968 to 1969. In the latter year the Les Paul Deluxe took its place, the first newly named Les Paul model in 14 years.

The Deluxe was prompted by calls from Gibson's marketing people, who were being told by music dealers that players wanted the gold-top model with humbucking pickups (rather than the single-coil P90s of the existing re-issue model). But it seems that Gibson wanted to keep the separate visual identity of a guitar with smaller pickups, and so a compromise had to be reached.

Jim Deurloo had joined Gibson back in 1958 as a rim-sander, and worked his way up through the factory. By 1969 he was heading the pattern shop at Kalamazoo, and was given the task of providing the Deluxe with humbuckers. . . without incurring new tooling costs. His only solution was to fit a humbucking pickup into a P90 space. He considered a few options, eventually using an Epiphone mini-humbucking pickup, of the type that appeared on Epiphone models such as the Riviera and Sorrento semi-acoustics and the Crestwood and Wilshire solids.

Gibson had acquired Epiphone in about 1957. According to Ted McCarty, who was president at the time of the purchase, Gibson thought that for the $200,000 asking price they were buying only Epiphone's string-bass business. What they actually ended up with was virtually the entire Epiphone company: guitars, parts, machinery and all. "We only discovered that when they shipped the whole thing back here in a big furniture truck," says McCarty, who had to rent space in another building in Eleanor Street in Kalamazoo so that Epiphone parts could be prepared before final assembly at Parsons Street. "I put Ward Arbanas in charge of it, and we made the Epiphone guitars exactly the way Epiphone made them, with every detail exact," says McCarty.

Production of Gibson-made Epiphones was underway in 1959 – by 1961 totally at Parsons Street – and many fine guitars were produced. Gibson maintained the names of Epiphone's best-known models, while others were new Epiphone 'equivalents' of Gibson models, such as the Casino which was very similar to a Gibson ES330 (but with an Epiphone logo, of course).

By 1969 the Epiphone line was being run down, and it seems that the most likely reason for this was because by then Epiphone prices more or less matched those of Gibson. The result was that customers would opt for the better-known name of Gibson, meaning a drop in demand for Epiphones. Again, cost-consciousness decreed that something had to be done, and by 1970 Gibson phased out US production of Epiphones and applied the brandname to cheaper guitars imported from oriental factories.

For the Gibson Les Paul Deluxe, Jim Deurloo accommodated the mini-humbucker by taking a P90 cover, cutting a hole in it, and dropping in the small Epiphone unit. . . of which Gibson now had surplus stocks. The result pleased everyone: the look was traditional, the pickup was a humbucker, and no extra tooling costs had been incurred. "The first ones were

very crudely done," recalls Deurloo of the cut-out made in the P90 covers, "but later we did tool up for it, and routed and drilled the cover."

At first the Deluxe was only available with a gold top, but gradually sunbursts and other colors were introduced, and it lasted in production until the mid-1980s. It appeared on Gibson's September 1969 pricelist, its year of introduction, at $425.

The gold-top model, which as you may remember had been re-issued in 1968 with P90s and a Tune-o-matic bridge, had been dropped on the release of the Deluxe in 1969. But a new gold-top re-issue was launched by Gibson around 1971, this time with the wrap-over bar-shaped bridge/tailpiece of the type fitted to the second version of the original 1950s model. It also had the narrow binding in the body cutaway characteristic of 1950s Les Pauls (see pp26/27), prompting suggestions that Gibson were using up old bodies. This gold-top lasted until about 1972, but did not appear on the company's pricelists.

NAMING THE PARTS

By this time Gibson had taken the rather egotistical step of applying the company logo to their pickups, and indeed the P90 units fitted to the 1971 gold-top model, among other Gibson electrics, bear this mark. The practice resulted in a ridiculous situation where dealers who wanted to stock spares would have to order two completely different units for two-humbucker guitars. This was necessary so that when the polepieces of the neck and bridge units correctly faced forwards and backwards, the Gibson logo did not appear upside-down on one of the pickups. The logo was phased out during the 1970s.

As we've seen, Les Paul's ideas on guitar design did not necessarily coincide with the guitar styles that Gibson felt would be commercially successful. Back in the 1950s and 1960s one of Paul's more out-of-step tastes was for low-impedance pickups. Today, low-impedance elements are more often used in pickup design thanks to improvements in associated components, but back then Paul was largely on his own. The vast majority of electric

Body sandwich close-up (above)
Some changes in construction were instituted at Gibson around 1970. The thin stripe seen on the body edge is evidence of a technique called 'cross-banding', used between about 1969 and 1973, where a strengthening sheet of maple is inserted between a sandwich of upper and lower blocks of mahogany.

Volute close-up (above)
Another change made around 1970 was the addition of this lump, or 'volute', where the rear of the neck meets the headstock, again intended to strengthen a weak area. It lasted until about 1981.

Gibson catalog 1968 (above)
During the late 1960s demand for the discontinued Gibson Les Pauls had been growing among guitarists, especially blues-rock players. This brochure officially records Gibson's reaction to such demand: the re-introduction in original-design Les Paul models.

Gibson ad 1970 (left)
Here are the two Les Paul models that Gibson were forced to re-introduce in 1968, the Custom and the gold-top. "The demand for them just won't quit," says the harassed guitar-maker from Kalamazoo.

Gold-top 1968 (left)
One of the two Les Paul models that Gibson re-introduced in 1968, the gold-top lasted only until 1969 with a Tune-o-matic bridge. In fact the guitar shown is a curious example, perhaps from early production, as the headstock is without the 'Les Paul Model' logo one would usually expect. Instead it bears the 'crown' inlay of the type used on the earlier SG/ Les Paul Standard, while the truss-rod cover, usually blank, has a 'Les Paul' inscription.

Deluxe 1970 *(right)*
The gold-top of 1968-69 was
effectively replaced by the Les Paul
Deluxe model, launched in 1969. The
Deluxe's use of Epiphone mini-
humbucker pickups was unusual,
lending a distinctive look and a brighter
sound than the Les Paul models
equipped with familiar Gibson
humbuckers. The Deluxe began its life
only in gold-top finish; later, sunbursts
and other colors were offered.

Normal pickups *(above)*
Most Deluxes have pickups with a
small metal cover sitting in a single
plastic surround, as can be seen on this
1980 example.

43

'Ringed' pickups *(above)*
Early Deluxe pickups had mini-
humbuckers fitted in cut-out P90
covers. Some, like those on this
1970 example, have an extra
ring around the plastic cover.
Designed to mask small tooling
blemishes, the rings were known
unofficially at the Gibson factory as
'goof hiders'.

Custom c1968
(left)
This was the other Les Paul model re-
introduced in 1968, partnering the
revitalized gold-top. There was some
discussion at Gibson about making the
'new' Custom in white, as the SG/Les
Paul Custom had been, but eventually
it was decided to release it in black,
like the original 1950s model. However,

the inclusion of three humbuckers on
the 1957-61 version had never been
too popular with players, and so the
1968 re-release saw the instigation of
two humbuckers as the normal pickup
layout. Despite this change, limited
numbers of three-humbucker Customs
have been made at various times,
starting in the 1970s. (The tuners on
this example are non-original.)

guitars and guitar-related equipment was and still is high-impedance.

Paul described his reasons for working with low-impedance pickups to Jon Sievert in *Guitar Player* magazine in December 1977: "I figured out very early through my study of electronics that low impedance was the way to go. I figured that if the telephone company used it, that's the way to go. If you walked into a professional recording studio and someone handed you a high-impedance mike, you'd think he was nuts."

He went on to explain the oft-quoted advantages of low-impedance pickups: they don't, as he put it, "pick up the sound of the cash register or the neon lights" – which is simply a consequence of their low power – and they can be used effectively with very long runs of cable without great loss of high frequencies. But the real bonus to be gained from low-impedance pickups is their wide and all-encompassing tonal characteristics – although of course this isn't necessarily to everyone's taste.

Low impedance pickups need to have their power boosted at some point before the signal reaches the amplifier, unless the player is direct-injecting ('DI-ing') the guitar straight into a recording studio mixer or some other device able to accept low-impedance signals. Paul used this DI-ing method, and the full sonic range available from his low-impedance pickups partly explains the excellent tonal clarity he achieved on record.

IMPEDANCE LOWDOWN

When Paul had gone to Gibson in 1967 to discuss the revival of Les Paul guitars, he'd talked with great passion about his beloved low-impedance pickups, and how Gibson should use them on some of their instruments. Bruce Bolen was at the meeting, and says, "Although he was talking around the fact that we should re-introduce the Les Paul, he had a new item that he was trying to present to Gibson, the low impedance pickup. He had made a couple of special guitars with them on and I was asked to compare these to our humbuckings. A lot of people in that particular era didn't have a feel for what Les was trying to present there. So Gibson were

asking to use my ears – and it was such a revelation on frequency response."

So in 1969 along came the first wave of Gibson Les Paul models with low-impedance pickups: the Les Paul Professional; the Les Paul Personal; and the Les Paul Bass. While Bolen remembers some initial prototypes with flat-topped bodies and a very thin profile, it seems that CMI boss Maurice Berlin said he wanted these proposed models to be about half-an-inch bigger around the body outline, so that they would be more visible on stage and TV screen. Despite the suitability of the guitars' electronics to recording studios, and the fact that the extra weight would mean a very heavy guitar, this larger size was adopted for the production versions of the Personal and Professional models.

The Personal was, as the name implied, in keeping with one of Paul's own modified Les Paul guitars, even copying the feature of a microphone socket on the top edge of the guitar. The general need for such a facility could not have been widespread.

DECADE & PHASE

The Personal and Professional had a complex array of controls, and reading Gibson's instruction leaflet for the instruments reinforces the impression that these guitars were built with recording engineers rather than guitarists in mind. Familiar volume, bass, treble and pickup selector were augmented by an 11-position 'Decade' control, "to tune high frequencies," a three-position tone selector to create various in- and out-of-circuit mixes, and a pickup in-/out-of-phase switch. The Personal also provided a volume control for that handy on-board microphone input.

Both guitars required connection via the special cord supplied, which had an integral transformer to boost the output from the low-impedance stacked-coil humbucking pickups to a level suitable for use with normal high-impedance amplifiers. "Otherwise this instrument will not function correctly," warned the instructions. It is not documented how many Personal or Professional owners turned up at a concert without their Low Impedance Transformer Cord and were forced to entertain the audience with jokes, a cappella songs, and so on.

Doubtless those who persevered with these complicated new toys were able to persuade the guitars to "produce literally all modern tonalities and bring forth sounds never before achieved on an electric guitar," as Gibson's leaflet gushed. But the guitars were not a great success, and did not last long in the Gibson line. Their rather somber brown color, achieved with a natural mahogany finish, could not have helped in an era when competitors were busily turning out simple guitars in bright colors.

The Les Paul Bass was the first Gibson bass guitar to bear Les Paul's name, and was similar to the low-impedance guitars. It featured two angled, black-cover pickups, but only the phase switch and the tone selector from the guitars' circuitry. It too required a special cord, and similarly lasted only a very short time in production.

Gibson's pricelist from September 1969 has the three Les Paul low-impedance models listed as follows: Personal, $645; Professional, $485; and Bass, $465. Gibson also produced a special LP12 combination amplifier/loudspeaker and LP1 amplifier, both with switchable high/low impedance for use with the guitars (and enabling guitarists to use any standard connecting lead). These are shown on the September 1970 Gibson amplification pricelist at $1110 for the LP12 and $505 for the LP1.

In 1970 Gibson launched a very peculiar instrument, the Les Paul Jumbo. This was a flat-top acoustic guitar with round soundhole and a cutaway. It had a low-impedance pickup installed in the top and a row of body-mounted controls (volume, treble and bass, the dainty 11-way 'Decade' control, and a bypass switch designed to cut the tone controls from the circuit). Very few Les Paul Jumbos were made, and it's not difficult to see why. It made a final appearance on Gibson's November 1971 pricelist, at $610.

The company made their second attempt at a range of low-impedance instruments in 1971. First, they scaled down the body size of the Professional/Personal style, virtually to that of a normal Les Paul, and gave it a contoured back. Second, they located the still-necessary transformer into the guitar itself, and provided a switch on the guitar to give either low-impedance output or normal high-impedance output. Third, they re-titled the guitar to the seemingly more appropriate Les Paul Recording. The bass model underwent similar modifications, and although now called the Les Paul Triumph Bass it was still simply tagged in some Gibson literature as the Les Paul Bass.

Gibson's pricelist for June 1971 shows the Les Paul Recording at $625 and the Les Paul Triumph Bass at $515. This second wave of low-impedance models lasted until the end of the 1970s. Bruce Bolen summarises the lack of success of the low-impedance models as a matter of taste: "The high end was so clean on those guitars that they just didn't have enough harmonic distortion to relate to the rock players."

SIGNATURE TUNES

Gibson's final fling with low-impedance pickups was reserved for the company's 'thinline' electric guitar design, a narrow, semi-hollowbody style of guitar that had begun with the classic Gibson ES335 in 1958. That instrument came complete with a central block of timber inside the body on which to mount the pickups and bridge, reducing feedback and providing the guitar with an interesting blend of solidbody and hollowbody tones.

In 1974 the company launched the two-pickup Les Paul Signature guitar and the single-pickup Les Paul Signature Bass, in the thinline style. As Bruce Bolen explains, "It was basically an asymmetric 335, although it didn't have the full center block like a 335." It did have a block under the bridge, however, and in this sense was similar to Gibson's ES330 model (and indeed the 335 had lost its full center block for a short time at this period). While a few early Signatures appeared with round-end pickups similar to the stacked low-impedance units found on the Professional, Personal and Recording, most Signatures came with white rectangular low-impedance pickups containing Gibson's normal side-by-side humbucking coils.

Personal c1969 (below)
This strange model was, as the name implies, based on Les Paul's personal guitar. Along with the Professional also released in 1969, the Personal was designed around low impedance pickups, which give a wide frequency range but require boosting for use with normal amplifiers. This meant using a special cord supplied with the guitar.

Personal close-up (left)
This microphone socket was fitted to the top edge of the Personal's body, copying a facility which Les Paul used on his own stage guitar. He would plug in a gooseneck-mounted microphone, enabling him to talk while walking around the stage. The idea did not catch on.

Gibson ad 1974 (right)
A crazed-looking gent plays the new low impedance Signature model: "The first thin-line, semi-acoustic Les Paul ever," says the copy, and continues, "If you do any recording, you'll appreciate the two jack outputs Les designed into the guitar. One for you, and one for the engineer."

48

Recording c1972 (above)
The unpopular Personal and
Professional models gave way in 1971
to the Les Paul Recording. Controls
included phase, hi/lo impedance and
11-way tone 'Decade'.

Gibson catalogs 1970s
(left)
A color page from the brochure
of British Gibson agent Selmer (far
left) details the Recording model
and the Triumph Bass, while a 1970
US catalog shows the earlier Les
Paul Bass.

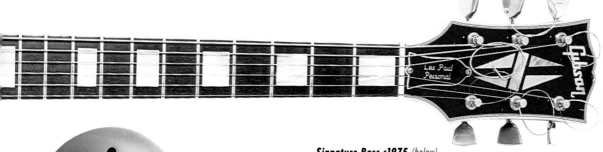

Signature Bass c1975 (below)
The bass version of the Signature had a
single low impedance pickup, but kept
the three-way impedance level switch.

47

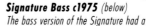

Signature c1976 (above)
The first and only semi-acoustic Les
Paul model, the Signature was

launched in 1974. Twin low impedance
pickups were linked to controls for
impedance level and phase in/out.

Gibson catalog 1970 (right)
These pages from a Gibson USA catalog
show the Les Paul Jumbo (far right),
which was a curious, shortlived model
with a cutaway acoustic body and low
impedance pickup, and the Les Paul
Professional (1969-71). This was
similar to the more expensive Personal,
but it lacked the microphone socket
and was fitted with nickel-plated rather
than gold-plated hardware.

Some of the Signature's controls were similar to those found on previous low-impedance models, but the 11-position 'Decade' control had shrunk to a three-position switch and lost its name. A notable inclusion on the Signature was two jack sockets – one on the side of the body for normal high-impedance output, and one on the face of the body for connection to low-impedance equipment, such as recording mixers. A similar facility was offered on the final version of the Recording model. The Signature models never really fired players' imaginations, and by the end of the 1970s had gone out of production. Gibson's February 1974 pricelist shows the Signature at $610 and the Signature Bass at $540.

In 1974 Gibson realized that it was 20 years since the first Les Paul Custom had appeared, so they celebrated by issuing a Custom with an appropriate 'Twentieth Anniversary' inlay at the 15th fret, in place of the normal blank position marker. This was the first Gibson anniversary model (and the only precursors in the electric guitar market were Gretsch's four Anniversary models of 1958, issued to celebrate the company's foundation 75 years earlier). The 20th Anniversary Les Paul Custom established an adroit marketing trend and a number of special anniversary edition Les Paul models have since appeared. As one ex-Gibson man puts it: "Whenever it was time for an anniversary, we made one."

By now Gibson employed around 600 people at its Kalamazoo factory, and produced some 300 guitars a day. Demand for guitars had increased during the early 1970s, and as a result the management of Gibson's parent company, Norlin, decided to build a second factory in Nashville, Tennessee, some 500 miles south of Kalamazoo.

No doubt many factors affected the choice of site, but one that was high on Norlin's list was the fact that Tennessee was a 'right to work' state – in other words unions existed but employees could choose whether or not to join. Michigan, and indeed a good deal of the north-eastern United States, had much stronger unions and established closed-shop arrangements, meaning obligatory union membership, along with generally higher worker's compensation and insurance rates.

Recent strikes at Gibson had cost Norlin dear, and so their new plant of 100,000 square feet at Nashville was constructed not only with increased production in mind, but also with a view to decreasing costs through advantageous labor deals.

Work began in 1974 on the new facility, five miles to the east of Nashville, and the factory eventually opened in June 1975. Training a new workforce took some time. Stan Rendell, then still Gibson president, says, "A limited number of people were transferred from Kalamazoo to Nashville in supervisory positions, but no workers were transferred. So everybody there had to be hired and trained, and that takes time. I think a Les Paul guitar took on average eight or ten man-hours of labor. So if you're going to make, say, 100 guitars a day you would need maybe 125 or more direct labor people – and that's without all the support personnel. It takes time to train the management, the workers, everybody. So we shipped some key people down there."

KALAMAZOO VS. NASHVILLE

The original intention was to keep both Kalamazoo and Nashville running, and that the new Nashville plant would produce only acoustic guitars. Stan Rendell says that trying to build acoustics and electrics in the same factory is a bit like trying to build trucks and automobiles in the same place. They need different kinds of attention at different stages in their fabrication.

"The real challenge," says Rendell, "is to schedule a flow of work through the factory so that everybody is kept busy. For example, the amount of work needed to finish an electric guitar is tremendous, whereas with an acoustic guitar about all you've got to do is put on strings and machine heads. So the types of guitars flowing through final assembly at any one time make a big difference to the workload. What I wanted to do was to try to specialise and remove the flat-top acoustic guitars out of the mainstream at Kalamazoo, and get a group of people who lived and breathed nothing but acoustic guitars at Nashville."

Unfortunately, the new acoustic project allocated to Nashville was the Mark series, some of the least successful of Gibson's flat-tops. The guitars were fraught with technical and constructional problems, and as one ex-employee puts it, "The Mark series was a fiasco." With this failure, management then decided to transfer to Nashville production of the bulk of the Les Paul range, by far the most successful part of the solidbody line at the time. Ken Killman, manager of Gibson's Customer Service department, told *Melody Maker* in 1975: "During the early 1960s we couldn't sell solidbodies at all; now the Les Paul line is the largest seller of the lot."

Kalamazoo had always been what is called a 'soft tool' factory, which means that the machines and fixtures used to make the guitars could be modified and adapted at will as circumstances dictated. Nashville started life as a 'hard tool' facility, which means that it had a lot of heavy machines and fixtures on which the settings were never changed.

To characterize the two factories that Gibson ran during the remaining years of the 1970s and into the early 1980s, Nashville was set up to produce very large quantities of a handful of models, whereas Kalamazoo was more flexible and had the potential to specialize in small runs. Nashville was thus the obvious choice to produce the highest volume lines of Gibson's solidbody line at the time, the Les Paul Custom and Les Paul Deluxe, along with various other solid models.

As if to highlight the contrast between the two plants' capabilities, Gibson introduced two new Les Paul models in 1976. First was the Pro Deluxe, effectively a Deluxe with P90 pickups and an ebony fingerboard. It was produced in large quantities at Nashville.

The other new model in 1976 was The Les Paul, a spectacular limited edition notable for its use of fine woods for virtually the entire instrument. Many parts that on a normal electric guitar would be made from plastic were hand-carved from rosewood. These included the pickguard, backplates, control knobs and truss-rod cover. Raw bodies and necks of attractive maple and an ornate ebony and rosewood fingerboard were produced at Gibson's Kalamazoo factory. Further work on the multiple colored binding, abalone inlays and handmade wooden parts was continued at the workshop of freelance luthier

Dick Schneider, about a mile from the factory in Kalamazoo. Schneider worked on The Les Pauls together with his brother Donnie and Abe Wechter from Gibson.

Very few The Les Pauls were made, and while an obvious four-figure misprint in Gibson's own records precludes an exact total, there were well under 100 produced, from 1976 to 1979 (primarily in the first year). During this time Schneider moved away from Kalamazoo, and Gibson workers report that some later examples of The Les Paul were therefore produced entirely at the Gibson factory. As the limited stocks of Schneider's handmade wooden parts ran out so normal plastic items were substituted, along with less ornate binding.

Each example of The Les Paul had a numbered oval plate on the back of the headstock. Bruce Bolen remembers flying to Hollywood to present number 25 to Les Paul, just prior to the 1977 Grammy Awards ceremony where Paul and Chet Atkins received a Grammy for their "Chester & Lester" album.

"The Les Paul was a fun project," remembers Stan Rendell. "They were gorgeous guitars, the wood was so beautiful. I remember saying nothing to CMI about it until we had it done. We showed it at NAMM and I remember Les Propp, president of CMI at the time, saying, How much you gonna charge for that guitar? Well, I says, it's 3000 bucks. And he choked," laughs Rendell. That tag put The Les Paul at four times the cost of its nearest Les Paul rival on the June 1976 pricelist, the $739 Custom.

STANDARD: IT'S OFFICIAL

It seems that there had not been enough fun projects to maintain Stan Rendell's interest as president of Gibson, and in November 1976 he resigned. After various short-stay presidents, Marty Locke moved over from CMI's Lowrey organ business to head up Gibson in 1980.

In the mid to late 1970s Gibson indulged in more theme and variation within the Les Paul range, but little innovation. In 1975 the Standard was introduced. It had 'Standard' stamped on its truss-rod cover, at last making official a name used inconsistently and inaccurately by

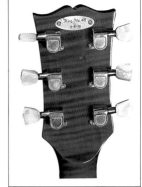

50

The Les Paul close-ups (right)
Gibson president Stan Rendell acquired
some beautiful figured maple in Austria
that was put to good use for the
overtly attractive The Les Paul. This
exquisite back (right) has the figure
enhanced by the transparent red finish.
The Les Paul was made in very limited
numbers, and each carried a numbered
plaque (far right) on the rear of the
headstock. Shown here is number 48,
completed in March 1978.

Pro Deluxe 1980 (below)
Introduced in 1976, the Les Paul Pro
Deluxe was in effect a Deluxe with P90
pickups and an ebony fingerboard.

The Les Paul 1978 (below)
Clever work by luthier Dick Schneider on carved rosewood parts (including knobs and pickguard) and crafted binding contributed to a $3000 price-tag.

Gibson ad 1978 (above)
Several features of the 25/50 are extolled here, including the fine-tuning tailpiece, brass nut, coil-tap switch and high-output pickups.

Artisan 1982 (right)
The distinguishing visual feature of the Custom-derived Artisan (1977-82) was its ebony fingerboard with ornate position markers. The floral inlay design looked more like the sort of thing one would expect to find on a Martin acoustic than a Gibson electric. An earlier version of the Artisan came with three pickups.

20th Anniversary 1974 (right)
This was Gibson's first commemorative Les Paul, issued to celebrate the passing of 20 years since the birth of the Custom model. Not that the result was ostentatious: some small lettering on the position block at the 15th fret reads 'Twentieth Anniversary'. So it's a pity that the pickup layout is pure 1974, rather than echoing that of 1954.

25/50 Anniversary 1979 (right)
Gibson's second anniversary Les Paul was issued as a double-headed celebration. The '25' refers to Les Paul's 25-year association with Gibson, implying that the idea if not the guitar appeared in 1977. The '50' indicates Paul's 50th year in the music business. (The pickguard has been removed from this example to show off its figured top.)

51

Gibson and by outsiders for various older Les Pauls. The new Standard was a straightforward sunburst model with two humbuckers, later appearing in a variety of finishes.

The 25/50 Les Paul was intended to celebrate Les Paul's 25th year with Gibson (presumably it had been planned for 1977) and his 50th year in the music business. The silver and gold themes generally associated with these anniversaries were reflected in the guitar's chrome- and gold-plated hardware, while Chuck Burge in Gibson's R&D (research and development) department designed the special intricate inlay in pearl and abalone on the guitar's headstock. The guitar bore a three-digit edition number on the back of the headstock as well as a standard serial number, and Les Paul was presented with number 001 at a party given in his honor by Gibson, who launched the instrument in 1978.

Despite its relatively high price (around $1200) the Kalamazoo-made 25/50 sold well, bringing into sharp focus for Norlin the ready market for more costly Les Paul models. But management was also swayed by the opinions of Gibson's salespeople as to the market's requirements: an example from this period is the Les Paul KM model, one of a series of six uninspiring instruments made for a southern sales region. The 'KM' almost certainly stands for 'Kalamazoo Model'.

Tim Shaw joined Gibson in 1978, having worked in California and in Kalamazoo as a guitar repairer and maker. His first few months were spent in Gibson's pickup plant in Elgin, Illinois, but by early 1979 he was working with Bruce Bolen in R&D at Kalamazoo, and together with Chuck Burge and Abe Wechter built prototypes and artists' instruments and worked on new designs.

Shaw recalls that one of the first prototypes he was involved with became the Les Paul Artist model, which used a package of active electronics originally developed for Gibson's RD models. Synthesisers were becoming big business in the late 1970s, and Norlin figured that a hook-up with one of the synth field's most famous names, Moog, might re-capture some of the ground that guitars were losing to the new keyboards. Gibson's RD line was issued in 1977, but did not prove popular. Many guitarists dislike active circuitry, and this

was a major factor in the downfall of the RD series. Gibson believed the radical styling was more to blame, and moved to combine the RD technology with traditional designs.

"In 1979 Gibson decided to expand the RD concept into two of their more mainstream series, the ES and the Les Paul," Shaw explains. "We had to re-design the circuit board, because the original RD board is too big for almost anything. So we made it into two boards, which still meant we had to take a lot of wood out of the Artist guitars. But something I didn't fully appreciate until later was that guitar players are really conservative folks, and nobody really wanted a Les Paul that did all that. Somebody once said that with one of those Artists you were a flick of a switch away from total disaster."

The Artist hobbled on to 1981, when it was quietly dropped. A happier project was the Les Paul Heritage Series, one of the first conscious attempts to try to make Les Pauls in a way that many people thought was no longer possible at Gibson. A reasonably healthy market had been building since the late 1960s in so-called 'vintage' guitars (which until then had been called merely secondhand, used, or just plain old guitars). This was fuelled by the general feeling that Gibson didn't 'make them like they used to,' combined with the prominent use of older instruments by many of the most popular guitarists of the day.

NEW OLDIES

Some US dealers who specialized in older instruments had already begun to order selected models with 'vintage' appointments from Gibson's Kalamazoo plant, which since the onset of the Nashville factory was beginning to lean more heavily toward shorter, specialized runs of guitars. Jim Deurloo, by then plant manager at Kalamazoo, remembers dealers such as Leo's and Guitar Trader ordering these special 'vintage' style Les Paul models.

"They were selected from the line, and custom-built to some degree," says Deurloo of the dealer specials. "That was at a time when we weren't making a vintage looking instrument. We were making what was in the catalogue at the time, and not the guitar with the washed-out top," he continues. "I remember that Guitar Trader selected each top, and they were very picky about the colour."

Meanwhile, during 1979 Chuck Burge started building prototypes for the Heritage Series Les Pauls. Tim Shaw remembers: "They were our first stab at asking questions like, What's the best this guitar ever was? Are we building it like that now? And if not, why not? Management didn't want to hear that at first, so we fought tooth and nail to do it."

The R&D team used a 1954 pattern sample for the carving of the body top, they changed neck construction to three-piece mahogany, disposed of then-current production oddities such as the volute below the back of the headstock, and moved a little closer to older pickup specs. Pretty timber was selected for the tops of these new Heritage Series Les Pauls.

Bruce Bolen, head of R&D by then, managed to persuade Norlin to put the 'vintage'-flavoured Heritages into production – not as standard Les Pauls, however, but rather as separate, premium items, touted as 'limited editions' and not included on the company's general pricelist. Launched in 1980, the two models in the Heritage Series were the Heritage Standard 80 and the Heritage Standard 80 Elite, the latter with an ebony fingerboard and 'quilted' top.

Whether as a result of the influence of the Heritage models or a general awareness of market demands, Gibson began at this time to rectify some of the general production quirks instituted in the 1970s, removing the volute, for example, and gradually reverting to one-piece mahogany necks.

The July 1980 pricelist shows six Les Paul models: the Artist ($1299), the Artisan (a sort of decorated Custom, at $1099), the Custom ($949, or with nickel-plated hardware $899), the Pro Deluxe ($889), the Standard ($849), and the Deluxe ($799).

According to some of the employees at Gibson, it seems likely that by about 1980 Norlin had decided to sell Gibson. A later report in *Music Trades* magazine says that by 1981 Norlin Industries had incurred excessive debt through substantial losses in its music divisions, which forced the sale of its profitable technology and beer divisions in 1982. As well as Gibson and Gibson Accessories, Norlin's music divisions included Lowrey organs, Moog synthesisers, and a 'Band & Orchestral' division.

As an example of Norlin's falling income, Gibson sales fell 30 per cent in 1982 alone, to a total of $19.5 million, against a high in 1979 of $35.5 million. Of course, Gibson was not alone in this decline. The guitar market in general had virtually imploded, and most other American makers were suffering in broadly similar ways. Their costs were high, economic circumstances and currency fluctuations were against them, and Japanese competitors increasingly had the edge.

Norlin's overall losses in its music divisions were high, according to a 1982 message to shareholders from chairman Norton Stevens: "The operating loss was $11 million before a goodwill write-off of $22.6 million," he said. Norlin had "lean music businesses whose break-even has been reduced significantly in the last few years," continued Stevens, putting a brave face on the company's position. He claimed that Norlin's objective was "to put our capital base to work for growing future earnings". By 1984 Stevens was off the Norlin board.

Norlin relocated some of its sales, marketing, administration and finance personnel from Chicago to Nashville around 1980. All the main Gibson production was now handled at the Nashville plant, while Kalamazoo had become a specialist factory making custom orders, banjos and mandolins. Plant manager Jim Deurloo told André Duchossoir for *Disc International* magazine in 1982: "The plant is now mainly manufacturing specific models that we call 'custom shop editions' built in small runs of 25 to 100, sometimes more. Kalamazoo is more of a giant custom job shop, and we are proud of our heritage and workmanship."

CALAMITY IN KALAMAZOO

In July 1983 Gibson president Marty Locke informed Jim Deurloo that the Kalamazoo plant would close. The last production at Kalamazoo was in June 1984, and the

Heritage Series Standard 80 1980 (right)
This model gives the first indication that Gibson were responding to the charge that Les Pauls were not what they used to be. More care was spent on the Heritage models, and a few constructional oddities that had developed in the 1970s were sidestepped. There were two models in the Heritage Series: the Standard, with a pleasantly figured top, and Elite, which was equipped with fancier curly maple.

54

Spotlight Special 1983 (above)
Gibson used some surplus parts to produce the distinctive Spotlight Special, assembling a central block of walnut (left over from a discontinued model) between outer pieces of figured maple. This particular example uses some especially spectacular maple that exhibits unusually strong grain 'waves' running from top to bottom, roughly parallel to the walnut block, as well as side-to-side figure patterns.

Gibson ad 1982 (left)
To celebrate 30 years since the Les Paul's first appearance in 1952, Gibson chose the later appointments of Tune-o-matic bridge and humbuckers for their 30th Anniversary gold-top. This prompted the ad copywriter to describe it as "30 years of the electric guitar in the electric guitar that made history".

Gibson catalog 1981
(left)
On display are the LP XRI and XRII, which were rather unexciting models devised by one of Gibson's regional sales teams. The XRII had a flat, un-carved top and followed the contemporary trend for coverless humbuckers. Both models were shortlived.

Standard 1980 *(above)*
The Standard wasn't many years old before Gibson began to offer color options, such as this green example.

Artist 1979 *(below)*
Gibson's RD solids introduced in 1977 met with little success: they had relatively complex electronics and an unusual design. So Gibson decided to use their circuitry but in the familiar environment of a Les Paul, launching the Artist in 1979. The knobs control volume, bass and treble, the switches brightness, expansion and compression.

Spotlight close-up *(left)*
The Spotlight Special was put together in the Custom Shop at Gibson's Nashville factory. It bears the Shop's stamp on the rear of the headstock, along with a special three-digit serial number (after '83' which indicates the year of production).

plant closed three months later, after more than 65 years' worthy service since the original building had been erected by Gibson. It was an emotional time for the managers and workers, many of whom had worked in the plant for a considerable time.

One employee says that people there knew the closure was inevitable. "You added it all up, and the Kalamazoo factory was falling apart, a very old building, steeped so heavily in tradition and history. The Nashville plant was brand new, in 17 acres, a very beautiful facility. . . What it boils down to is that the business could not support the two facilities, and there was only really one choice." This observer notes too that the business would, of course, be easier to sell with just the Nashville plant and its more amenable labor relations and costs.

Tim Shaw also recalls those last years. "Jim Deurloo, to his great credit, had fought a hard battle to keep Kalamazoo open, and he lost. But when the announcement came down he got the entire factory together and said words to the effect of: Look, they've made the decision to close this place. You people have been with the company for a long time, and I'm very sorry that it's worked out this way. But you're all professionals, you've worked here a long time, you have a heritage to be proud of, and as we down-size and as we close I want you to remain professionals; basically, I want you to go out and smile.

"And I think to a large part, they did," Shaw continues. "But it hurt every time you looked around on a Friday and 30 to 60 people would disappear. I think Deurloo did all that was humanly possible in terms of keeping morale up and trying to set a tone in a very professional framework."

Some of the key people were offered positions in Nashville, but Deurloo, together with Marv Lamb, who'd been with Gibson since 1956, and J P Moats, a Gibson employee of equally long standing, decided to leave. They rented part of the Kalamazoo plant and started the Heritage guitar company in April 1985. They continue that business today: Heritage had 15 workers, a line of 35 models and produced some 1500 guitars in 1992. As Marv Lamb puts it, "We all grew up building guitars and

we didn't know too different. We could have searched for another job, but we wanted to do what we know how to do best."

SPOTLIGHT ON NASHVILLE

Although the emphasis at the Nashville plant was on large runs of a small number of Gibson models, this had to change gradually as it adjusted to its new role as the company's sole factory. For example, in 1983 Nashville produced the Spotlight Special, a limited run designed to use up various components.

Walnut had been left over from production of two models which had been discontinued – The Paul and The SG – and some narrow pieces of curly maple were spotted laying unused in the timber stock. Nashville managers combined these elements and adapted some rosewood headstock veneers and dark binding from a Chet Atkins model. The resulting concoction was the Les Paul Spotlight Special, with a body displaying a distinctive centre stripe of walnut between two maple 'wings.' The model seems to mark the start of an official Custom Shop at Nashville: it carries a 'Custom Shop' logo on the rear of the headstock, and an edition number showing the '83' date plus a three-digit serial.

A more enduring model also appeared in 1983, the Studio. Gibson decided they needed a cheaper Les Paul guitar and, as one person involved in the design puts it, "We stripped off the gingerbread." Primarily this meant no binding on the body or fingerboard, giving a basic, straightforward look. Bruce Bolen remembers a session to try to come up with a name for the model, which wasn't going too well until Bolen visited a recording studio that evening. "A little lightbulb came on in my head, and I thought, Let's call it the Studio. What could be more closely associated with Les than a studio?" By the mid 1980s Bolen had become vice president of marketing and R&D at Gibson, and in 1986 he left the company, after 19 years' sterling service.

The Les Paul Studio first appeared on the January 1983 pricelist at $699, which made it $300 cheaper than any other Les Paul at the time. Since its launch the Studio has been through several changes. It started with a body of normal size but, unusually for Gibson, of alder. However, aesthetic problems associated with the type of lacquer used prompted a quick change to Gibson's established maple/mahogany combination. This new body was around ⅛ inch thinner than other Les Pauls, which led to a reduction in production costs and weight.

Around 1986 some Studios began to appear with ebony rather than rosewood fingerboards – which on the face of it seems a luxurious feature for such a relatively cheap guitar. An insider explains the logic: "Gibson buys one grade of ebony, except that they don't really know how good it is until it's run through some machinery. The very black ebony is graded as top-quality and used for the finest instruments.

"Gibson does not dye any of their fingerboards, so they end up with an amount of less good ebony that has brown streaks in it, called C-grade ebony, and which can't be used for the more expensive guitars. So there's a whole family of instruments – and the Studio is the prime example because it's made in the largest quantity – which uses rosewood or C-grade ebony depending on availability. If there is a lot of C-grade ebony in the store, Gibson uses that. If they've run out of it for some reason, they use rosewood."

The earlier Studios have Gibson's standard fingerboard markers for cheaper models: dots. In about 1990 the fancier 'crown' type was adopted, a marketing decision to give the guitar a little more visual appeal. A version with bound neck and body, the Studio Standard, came along for a couple of years from 1984, while another variant was the Studio Custom with gold-plated hardware. By 1993 the Studio was still the least expensive Les Paul in the Gibson line, at $899.

GIBSON FOR SALE

You may recall that Norlin had put Gibson up for sale around 1980. By summer 1985 they finally found a buyer, and in January 1986 Henry Juskiewicz, David Berryman and Gary Zebrowski completed their purchase of the entire Gibson operation for an undisclosed sum (variously estimated in contemporary press reports as between $5 million and $10 million). By this time Norlin's main occupation was in the printing business, and Gibson was the last part of its once-large musical empire to be sold off.

Juskiewicz, Berryman and Zebrowski had first met while studying at the Harvard Business School in the late 1970s, since when Juskiewicz had been in engineering and investment banking, Berryman in accountancy, and Zebrowski in marketing. Also, crucially, Juskiewicz was an enthusiastic guitarist who loved Gibson instruments: "He's a fan," as one Gibson employee puts it.

The three had gone into business together, teaming up in 1981 to turn a failing electronics company in Oklahoma into a successful operation. When they bought Gibson in 1986 Juskiewicz became president, Berryman vice-president of finance and accounting, while Zebrowski continued to run their electronics business.

UNDER NEW MANAGEMENT

The most immediate effect of the new ownership was that a lot of people were fired, including the plant manager, quality control manager and many others. One could hardly expect this to be a popular first move. "It was pretty scary," admits one insider speaking in the early 1990s. "But Henry got what he was after. If you judge it on results, he brought the company back from the dead."

Juskiewicz admitted to a reporter in early 1986 that he was, as he described it, in the process of restructuring Gibson's production operation. He said the new Gibson set-up would be extremely aggressive in developing and introducing new products, and insisted that they would be more creative in merchandising and marketing than Gibson had ever been, with a more competitive pricing policy.

"It turned out well," says Juskiewicz today, "but I pretty much knew that it would be two years of sheer hell." As far as the ever-popular Les Paul models were concerned, Juskiewicz says that he inherited a poor relationship between Gibson and Les Paul himself. "Les obviously had a proprietary interest in the success of his guitars, and they'd killed them, so he was pretty annoyed. Les lives in New Jersey, and Kramer [a local

Sunburst 59 Re-issue 1987 *(left)*
The Heritage Series proved that Gibson could capitalize on their own past achievements, and five years later came the first of the company's Re-issue models. The 59 Re-issue was based on a Sunburst of 1959 vintage. Gradually specs of this and other Sunburst and gold-top Re-issues have improved to bring Gibson closer to the look and feel of the 1950s originals.

Hollow custom 1991 *(right)*
This was one of several unique instruments made for Malcolm Young of AC/DC by Roger Giffin of Gibson's West Coast Custom Shop. Young, normally a Gretsch fan, wanted something different, so Giffin made a series of trial electric-acoustic instruments. This one, a sort of hollow-Les-Paul-meets-Gretsch, was the fourth of the five which Giffin made.

Epiphone brochure 1991 *(above)*
The Gibson-owned Epiphone brand made guitars in Korea from the late 1980s, and this Epiphone Les Paul Standard was the first to bear the Les Paul marque.

58

35th Anniversary 1989 (right)
With a 20th, 25th and 30th behind them, Gibson aimed for the full set of celebratory models with this 35th Anniversary tribute to the 1954 Custom . . . and gave it the three-humbucker layout first seen in 1957. The anniversary inscription can be seen at the headstock, in the central bar of the split-diamond inlay.

Samurai 1989 (right)
This meticulously inlaid concoction was created at Gibson's Nashville Custom Shop by Greg Rich and Jim Triggs. It's part of a select line of what Gibson call their 'gallery quality' guitars, aimed at buyers of art. In 1992 the Custom Shop expected to make between 20 and 25 such instruments, with prices from $10,000 to $250,000 each.

Studio Lite 1992 (above)
Les Pauls have always suffered a weight problem and this model, in two guises, attempts a cure. An earlier offering had a Fender-style contoured body, while the version shown has 'chromite' (balsa) inserts in the body to lighten the load.

Gibson catalog 1988 (right)
The side view shows the contoured body which cut the weight of this Custom Lite (1987-89) and the early Studio Lite.

guitar maker] was constantly seeing him – he even did an MTV video saying how nice Kramer guitars were. So I established a rapport with Les early on, and that seemed to solve the problem. I listened to what he had to say: he wanted to see a lower-cost Les Paul instrument in our imported Epiphone line, for example, and we ended up doing that a few years into the business."

J T Riboloff joined Gibson in 1987, moving to Nashville from his home in California where he had operated as a guitar maker, repairer and restorer. He was hired for Gibson's Custom Shop, and soon became involved in work on new designs. Tim Shaw moved from the Custom Shop and R&D to an international role for Gibson, travelling often to Korea to help expand the company's Epiphone lines. He left in 1992, after 14 years' service with Gibson.

OLD LADIES & ELUSIVE SPECS

Two new Les Paul 'Re-issue Outfits' were launched in 1985. Gibson was now well aware of the continuing demand up at the monied end of the market for 'vintage' Les Pauls. The Heritage Series of 1980 had turned out to be only a half-hearted approach to a proper re-issue of the most celebrated old Les Pauls. The Re-issue Outfits were the next steps – backward and forward at the same time.

The February 1985 pricelist showed a gold-top Re-issue at $1299 and a Sunburst Re-issue at $1599 (well above the next most expensive Les Paul, the normal Custom at $1049). These were effectively high quality versions of the existing sunburst-finish and gold-top Standard models, the former with a selected curly maple top. Gradually since then Gibson have tried to improve the 'authenticity' of their Re-issues, driven by the persistent demands of customers seeking perfect duplication of those hallowed 1950s instruments.

"When I went to Gibson in '87 the Les Paul Re-issue was basically a Standard with a flame top," says Riboloff. "Slowly but surely they've let us get away with a little more." The basic Re-issue model is generally referred to as the 59 Re-issue because of its general proximity to a 1959-style Sunburst. Little 'corrections' have been made

since its introduction in 1985, including: a smaller-sized 'vintage' headstock; especially attractive figured maple for the top; the adoption of a new carving form to ape the original body contours; re-tooling of the neck for similar reasons; a slight reduction in the neck pitch; holly veneer for the headstock face; proper routing of the control cavity; early-style Tune-o-matic bridge; and the reinstatement of a longer and wider neck 'tongue' at the neck/body joint. This was the state of the 'new' 59 Re-issue introduced to the trade at the 1993 NAMM show, about as close as Gibson felt they could get to 1950s specs. But trying to determine those elusive specs is a job in itself.

Riboloff: "Researching the Re-issue, I probably looked at 25 different Les Paul Sunbursts from the 1958-60 era. They were all different," he laughs. For example, he says, no two headstocks were anything like the same. "The machine heads would be slightly further north or south, the wrist of the neck would start in a different area, the scroll was shorter, and the logo would be different," he says, exasperated. "They were soft-tooled back then, and so every one is different. Really, there is no super correct one to re-issue. So with these 25 to hand, we took the best attributes of each instrument – cosmetics, carving and all – and combined them."

Tim Shaw calls to mind the infamous Gibson 'old ladies' who did much of the hand-work in the factory at the time of the praised 1950s models. "They used to hand-sand the old ones a little bit differently every time," he says. "It used to tickle the hell out of me with all these people saying, Oh, the placement of the 'Gibson' logo has to be *right here*, and the 'Les Paul Model' *exactly there*. And I'd say, Those women who put the decals on, you think they measured? No!

"What's the correct specifications of an early Les Paul?" Shaw laughs at his unanswerable question, and concludes: "Who knows!"

One aspect of Les Pauls that leaves less room for argument is their weight. Some are, without doubt, heavier than others, but generally speaking a Les Paul is a heavy guitar. Gibson were determined to do something about this. The weight comes principally from the use of dense mahogany. J T Riboloff outlines the real extremes: "You can have two pieces the same size; one might weigh 5lbs, and the other 25lbs. The difference is due to the amount of minerals drawn into the wood as it grows, especially silica. Of course we don't use that extremely heavy stuff. That becomes fixtures, it's very useful for little wooden mallets," he laughs.

X-RAYS & THE SWISS CHEESE EFFECT

The new owners had inherited an earlier attempt to cut down the weight of the mahogany. Since about 1982 Nashville had drilled a series of small pockets into the mahogany section of Les Paul bodies, uncharitably called the 'Swiss cheese' effect by some observers. Of course once the maple top is in place these holes are invisible, except perhaps to touring musicians who take a keen interest in airport X-ray systems.

"I don't think it makes a bit of difference to the sound," says Tim Shaw concerning the 'Swiss cheese', "because the holes are too small to act as resonant cavities." And the new Gibson president, Henry Juskiewicz, amplifies: "It doesn't make any difference to the tonal characteristics of the model. We've tested this, and the absolutely critical part of the body to the sound of the instrument is the bridge area. If you do something up where the toggle switch is, say, it won't make any difference to the sound. The maple top is solid, of course, and a lot of the tonal characteristics come from that. So we're making a better guitar: it's more comfortable, and it still sounds good." The mahogany pockets continue to be applied to Les Paul models, with the exception of some of the Re-issues.

The first real attempt to deal with the Les Paul weight problem came in the form of a new model called the Les Paul Custom Lite, introduced in 1987. This had a contoured back that was pure Fender in style, and the timber lost in this sculpting reduced the guitar's weight and made it more comfortable to play. It was priced higher than the normal Custom, presumably as a result of extra production costs (on the September '87 list the basic models were pitched at $1170 for the Custom and $1249 for the Custom Lite), and it lasted to 1989.

Meanwhile, in 1988 Gibson introduced a similarly contoured version of their Les Paul Studio model, the Studio Lite (again, on the February '88 list, the Studio came at $909, the Studio Lite at $974). But a year earlier, Gibson had discovered 'chromite.' This is another name for balsa wood, derived from the first word of its Latin names, ochroma pyramidale and ochroma lagopus. Balsa has good resonating qualities and, despite a popular misconception, is certainly not cheap, being around four times more expensive than mahogany, for example. It was first used by Gibson in the form of body inserts to lighten the load of their new maple-top US1 electric of 1987.

Matthew Klein, a custom builder working in R&D at Gibson, had been trying out a hollowbody Les Paul, but found it did not have sufficient power nor the 'kick' associated with normal Les Paul models. Mike Voltz, another Gibson Custom Shop man, had been using balsa inserts in Gibson's Chet Atkins SST models, so Klein and Voltz began investigating the application of similar ideas to a Les Paul.

In 1990 the Studio Lite changed specification: it gained chromite (balsa) inserts, was given a normal flat back and a slimmer neck, and lost a couple of pounds in weight. A roughly D-shaped cut-out in the guitar body leaves the bridge and tailpiece connected to the back, with the space around filled by balsa inserts (which Gibson buys cut to required dimensions).

SLIMMER NECKS & BIRDSEYE FIGURE

J T Riboloff had found that a lot of players who were asking him to build special one-off guitars in the Custom Shop were requesting the slimmer-profile neck associated with the 1960 Sunburst model. Henry Juskiewicz noted the interest that an example of these one-offs caused at a NAMM show, and told Riboloff to start work on a production version. This appeared in 1990, and was called the Classic. A couple of years later the 60 Re-issue, a 1960-style Re-issue Sunburst, also appeared.

Juskiewicz had decided that the Classic needed to stand out a little from the rest of the line, so insisted on a '1960' logo on the guitar's pickguard, underlining the

Custom Plus 1992 *(below)*
Gibson began offering Plus and Premium Plus versions of some Les Pauls in 1992. These are similar to normal versions, but with more highly figured tops than usual, and often without a pickguard. The Premium Plus model has a more attractive top than the Plus, while the Plus is better than the relatively plain normal model.

Japanese ads 1990s *(right)*
Orville Gibson founded Gibson in the 19th century; now, 'Orville' is a Gibson brandname used for guitars made and sold only in Japan. The ads (center, right) are for Orville Les Paul Customs, one showing Les Paul himself clearly besotted. The other Japanese ad (left) is for the vintage-flavored Gibson Les Paul Classic, which was launched in 1990.

62

40th Anniversary 1991 *(left)*
Birthday time again, said Gibson, and inlaid the 15th fret to make this a 40th Anniversary model. The 1991 launch was a little premature, however; close reading of this book will reveal that no Les Paul models existed in 1951.

Standard 1990 *(right)*
Another example (see also page 55) of the range of colors in which the Standard is offered, contrasting with the familiar procession of sunbursts.

Studio Lite/MIII 1993 *(right)*
In 1991 Gibson launched a new MIII solid electric model with unusual body styling and versatile circuitry, but it did not prove popular. So the company quickly applied the MIII's electronics, along with its extra central single-coil pickup, to the less disturbing surroundings of a Les Paul. This resulted at first in the Classic/MIII (1991-92), and in 1992 the Studio Lite/MIII, as shown. It is still in production at the time of writing.

63

Deluxe Bass 1992 *(left)*
Bass guitars have not been a strong part of Gibson's inventory for some years, but in 1992 the company followed the so-called 'retro' trend for instruments with a hint of 1950s styling and introduced a new line of basses. They were given a Les Paul shape and became the first bass guitars to bear the Les Paul name since the Signature Bass was dropped at the end of the 1970s. There were initially three models, the basic Special Bass, the smarter Deluxe shown here, and the top-of-the-line Standard, with five-strings added later.

inspiration for its slim neck and 'vintage' sized headstock. The sound of the Classic was more modern thanks to powerful coverless humbuckers.

Riboloff's original intention had been to make the Classic with a rather plain top and 'faded' finish, resembling some of the less visually spectacular Sunbursts that players such as Jimmy Page would still occasionally take on stage. In 1992 a Classic Plus was added to the line, the 'Plus' indicating a more attractively figured top than the normal Classic – this was in fact timber deemed to be below the requirements of a Re-issue, but still good-looking enough to be worth a little extra.

In 1993 the grading of the tops became even more subdivided with the addition of a Classic Premium Plus (the best), a Classic Birdseye (with the distinctive rounded-figure maple generally referred to as 'bird's eye') and a Classic Premium Birdseye. Similar varieties were added to the Custom line when a Custom Plus and a Custom Premium Plus were offered in 1992 and 1993.

UN-GIBSON MIII

With the MIII model of 1991 Gibson launched a radically styled guitar with more flexible circuitry than normal, but it did not prove popular. In a move reminiscent of the marriage of RD and Artist ten years before, Gibson applied the electronics from the strange MIII to the more familiar environment of a Les Paul.

J T Riboloff had come up with the MIII idea, and originally wanted it to be a two-pickup guitar. Management pointed to the popularity of the humbucker/single-coil/humbucker arrangement elsewhere, and the MIII dutifully appeared in this three-pickup form. "My intention was to get every selection of the Stratocaster and every selection of the Les Paul from a five-way switch," says Riboloff. Unfortunately, Gibson's customers felt the design and the electronics of the MIII guitar were too 'un-Gibson', and did not rush to buy the instrument.

So the wiring was adapted into two Les Paul models, the Classic/MIII and the Studio Lite/MIII. Riboloff feels that the Studio Lite is better suited to the MIII sound, the

tone of the lightweight body sitting well with the expanded sonic possibilities of the circuitry. The Classic/MIII was dropped in 1992, while the Studio Lite/MIII was still on the catalogue in 1993.

LES PAULS FOR THE NINETIES

A fashion among some bass players for 1950s-styled instruments prompted Gibson to add three Les Paul basses to the range in 1992: the Deluxe, Special and Standard. They were designed primarily by Gibson's Phil Jones, and were the first bass guitars to carry the Les Paul name since the Triumph and Signature Basses of the 1970s. The new basses came in a variety of finishes and hardware styles, and in 1993 five-string versions were added, and active circuitry and a re-styled headstock were absorbed into the designs.

Gibson's April 1993 pricelist showed seven basic Les Paul guitars: Studio ($899); Special ($949); Studio Lite ($1099); Studio Lite/MIII ($1199); Standard ($1599); Classic ($2199); and Custom ($2199). There were also three basic Les Paul basses: Special ($1049); Deluxe ($1599); and Standard ($1649). The Historic Collection list showed six basic Les Paul models: 59 Sunburst Re-issue ($5059); 60 Sunburst Re-issue ($5059); 56 gold-top Re-issue ($2549); 57 gold-top Re-issue ($2549); Black Beauty 54 Custom Re-issue ($2399); and Black Beauty 57 Custom Re-issue ($2399 two pickups; $2399 three pickups).

As the latest Les Pauls come off the Gibson production line in Nashville, it's curious to observe that this design, dozens of years old, seems more than ever before to reflect the needs of contemporary musicians. Gibson at long last appears to have realized that, among the greatly increased competition of today's guitar market, they are uniquely placed to serve up the true, traditional flavor of the Les Paul model, but with all the benefits of the improvements made in modern manufacturing. More than 40 years after its first appearance in 1952 the Les Paul looks set for many new adventures, in the hands of succeeding generations of inspired guitarists and in the care of its industrious creators. Long may the Gibson Les Paul continue.

REFERENCE SECTION

There are four parts within the reference section that takes up the rest of this book. Starting on this page are the MODEL IDENTIFICATION CHARTS, explained below. Starting on page 80 is the main REFERENCE LISTING, which is explained on pages 78 and 79. On page 89 is a CHRONOLOGY showing all Gibson Les Paul models in the order that they were introduced. Closing the reference section on page 90 is an explanation of the methods that can be used for DATING Les Pauls.

THE MODEL IDENTIFICATION CHARTS that start here and continue to page 77 are designed to give information quickly and simply to help you distinguish between the main Les Paul models. Models are broken down first into nine main body shapes: Basic Les Paul (this page); SG

BASIC LES PAUL SHAPE

This is the classic style, and the symmetrical, waisted body with a single sharp cutaway was a traditional Gibson shape when applied to the very first Gibson Les Paul model, the gold-top of 1952. It was used widely since then, and is still in use today for a variety of models produced by Gibson and by many other makers in the USA and beyond.

○ Available at some periods. See page reference for more information.

	PRODUCTION PERIOD	PAGE REFERENCE	BOUND FINGERBOARD	ROSEWOOD	EBONY	MAPLE	METAL TUNER BUTTONS	PLASTIC TUNER BUTTONS	BOUND BODY	CARVED TOP
				FINGERBOARD				HEADSTOCK		BODY
C 'GOLD-TOP' 1st version (long trapeze)	1952-53	82	●	●				●	●	●
C 'GOLD-TOP' 2nd version (angled 1-piece bridge)	1953-55	82	●	●				●	●	●
C 'GOLD-TOP' 3rd version (white p/ups; 6-saddle bridge)	1955-57	82	●	●				●	●	●
C 'GOLD-TOP' 4th version (humbuckers)	1957-58	82	●	●				●	●	●
C 'SUNBURST'	1958-60	87	●	●				●	●	●
C 'GOLD-TOP' 5th version (6-saddle bridge; sep. tailpiece)	1968-69	82	●	●				●	●	●
C DELUXE	1969-84	82	●	●			○	●	●	●
C 'GOLD-TOP' 6th version (angled 1-piece bridge)	1971-72	82	●	●				●	●	●
C PRO DELUXE	1976-82	85	●		●		●		●	●
C STANDARD	1976-current	87	●	●			●		●	●
C KM	1979	83	●	●			●		●	●
C HERITAGE STANDARD 80	1980-82	82	●	●			●		●	●

(p72); Single-cut Junior/Special (p72); Double-cut Junior/Special (p74); Signature semis (p74); Professional/Personal (p74); 1970s basses (p76); 1990s basses (p76); and Acoustic body (p76).

Within the body shape divisions, models are further divided by the shape of the fingerboard markers, coded as follows: (C) crown markers; (D) dot markers; (B) block markers; (S) split-block markers; and (A) Artisan 'floral' markers (see below).

The table shows the production period of the model in question, plus a page reference to the main Reference Listing (where more detailed information can be found on each model). The table's main job is to provide identification clues based on various features of the fingerboard, headstock, body, pickups, pickguard, bridge and hardware, indicated as present by a solid black dot in the relevant column. An open dot means the feature was only available on that model for some periods; more information is given in the detailed listing at the page reference quoted.

FINGERBOARD MARKERS
Position indicators come in a variety of shapes on these Les Paul models.

C CROWN   D DOT   B BLOCK   S SPLIT-BLOCK   A ARTISAN

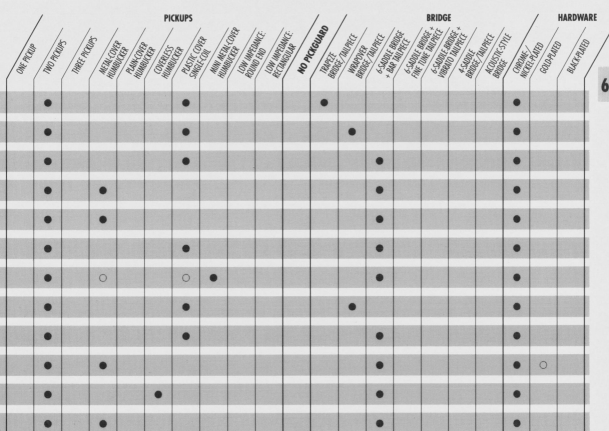

ONE PICKUP	TWO PICKUPS	THREE PICKUPS	METAL-COVER HUMBUCKER	PLAIN-COVER HUMBUCKER	COVERLESS HUMBUCKER	PLASTIC-COVER SINGLE-COIL	MINI METAL-COVER HUMBUCKER	LOW IMPEDANCE: ROUND END	LOW IMPEDANCE: RECTANGULAR	NO PICKGUARD	TRAPEZE BRIDGE/TAILPIECE	WRAPOVER BRIDGE/TAILPIECE	6-SADDLE BRIDGE + BAR TAILPIECE	6-SADDLE BRIDGE + FINE TUNE TAILPIECE	6-SADDLE BRIDGE + VIBRATO TAILPIECE	4-SADDLE BRIDGE/TAILPIECE	ACOUSTIC-STYLE BRIDGE	CHROME/NICKEL-PLATED	GOLD-PLATED	BLACK-PLATED
	•					•				•								•		
	•					•						•						•		
	•					•							•					•		
	•		•										•					•		
	•		•										•					•		
	•					•							•					•		
	•		○			○	•						•					•		
	•					•						•						•		
	•					•							•					•		
	•		•										•					•	○	
	•				•								•					•		
	•		•										•					•		

○ Available at some periods. See page reference for more information.

| | | PRODUCTION PERIOD | PAGE REFERENCE | BOUND FINGERBOARD | FINGERBOARD | | | METAL TUNER BUTTONS | HEADSTOCK | BODY |
					ROSEWOOD	EBONY	MAPLE		PLASTIC TUNER BUTTONS	BOUND BODY	CARVED TOP
C	HERITAGE STANDARD 80 ELITE	1980-82	83	●		●		●		●	●
C	'GOLD-TOP' 30th ANNIVERSARY	1982-83	88	●	●				●	●	●
C	SPOTLIGHT SPECIAL	1983	87	●	●				●	●	●
C	STUDIO	1990-current	87		●	○		●			●
C	'GOLD-TOP 57 RE-ISSUE' (humbuckers)	1985-current	82	●	●				●	●	●
C	'SUNBURST 59 RE-ISSUE'	1985-current	88	●	●				●	●	●
C	'SUNBURST' CMT	1986-89	87	●	●				●	●	●
C	CLASSIC	1990-current	80	●	●				●	●	●
C	'GOLD-TOP 56 RE-ISSUE' (white pickups)	1989-current	82	●	●				●	●	●
C	STUDIO LITE 2nd version (crown markers)	1990-current	87			●		●			●
C	CLASSIC/MIII	1991-92	80	●	●				●	●	●
C	40th ANNIVERSARY	1991 -current	88	●		●			●	●	●
C	CLASSIC CELEBRITY	1992	80	●		●			●	●	●
C	CLASSIC PLUS	1992-current	80	●	●				●	●	●
C	DE LUXE re-issue	1992-current	82	●	●			●		●	●
C	STUDIO LITE/MIII	1992-current	87			●		●			●
C	'SUNBURST 60 RE-ISSUE' (slim neck)	1992-current	88	●	●			●		●	●
C	CLASSIC BIRDSEYE	1993-current	80	●	●				●	●	●
C	CLASSIC PREMIUM PLUS	1993-current	80	●	●				●	●	●
C	CLASSIC PREMIUM BIRDSEYE	1993-current	80	●	●				●	●	●
D	LP XRI	1981-82	84		●			●			●
D	LP XRII	1981-82	84		●			●		●	
D	STUDIO	1983-90	87		●	○			●		●

	PICKUPS											BRIDGE							HARDWARE		
ONE PICKUP	TWO PICKUPS	THREE PICKUPS	METAL-COVER HUMBUCKER	PLAIN-COVER HUMBUCKER	COVERLESS HUMBUCKER	PLASTIC COVER SINGLE-COIL	MINI METAL-COVER HUMBUCKER	LOW IMPEDANCE: ROUND END	LOW IMPEDANCE: RECTANGULAR	**NO PICKGUARD**	TRAPEZE BRIDGE/TAILPIECE	WRAPOVER BRIDGE/TAILPIECE	6-SADDLE BRIDGE + BAR TAILPIECE	6-SADDLE BRIDGE + FINE TUNE TAILPIECE	6-SADDLE BRIDGE + VIBRATO TAILPIECE	4-SADDLE BRIDGE/TAILPIECE	ACOUSTIC-STYLE BRIDGE	CHROME/ NICKEL-PLATED	GOLD-PLATED	BLACK-PLATED
---	---	---	---	---	---	---	---	---	---	---	---	---	---	---	---	---	---	---	---	---
	●		●										●					●		
	●		●										●					●		
	●		●							●			●					●		
	●		●										●	○				●	○	
	●		●										●					●		
	●		●										●					●		
	●		●										●					●		
	●				●								●					●		
	●					●							●					●		
	●				●								●						○	●
		●			★	★				●			●					●		
	●		●										●						●	
	●				●								●						●	
	●				●								●					●		
	●						●						●					●		
		●			★	★							●						○	●
	●		●										●					●		
	●				●								●					●		
	●				●								●					●		
	●				●								●					●		
	●				●				●				●					●		
	●						●		●				●					●		
	●		●										●	○				●	○	

○ Available at some periods. See page reference for more information.

	Model	Production Period	Page Reference	Bound Fingerboard	Rosewood	Ebony	Maple	Metal Tuner Buttons	Plastic Tuner Buttons	Bound Body	Carved Top
						FINGERBOARD			**HEADSTOCK**	**BODY**	
D	STUDIO CUSTOM	1984-85	87		●	○			●		●
D	STUDIO STANDARD	1984-87	87	●	●	○			●	●	●
D	STUDIO LITE 1st version (dot markers)	1988-90	87			●		●			●
B	CUSTOM 1st version (black pickups)	1954-57	80	●		●		●		●	●
B	CUSTOM 2nd version (3 humbuckers)	1957-61	81	●		●		●		●	●
B	CUSTOM 3rd version (2 humbuckers)	1968-current	81	●		●	○	●		●	●
B	RECORDING 1st version (all controls on panel)	1971-77	85	●	●			●		●	●
B	CUSTOM '54 LTD EDITION'	1972-73	81	●		●		●		●	●
B	CUSTOM 20TH ANNIVERSARY	1974	88	●		●		●		●	●
B	THE LES PAUL	1976-79	88	●		●			●	●	●
B	RECORDING 2nd version (selector by neck pickup)	1977-79	85	●		●		●		●	●
B	ARTIST	1979-81	80	●		●		●		●	●
B	CUSTOM LITE	1987-89	81	●		●		●		●	●
B	35th ANNIVERSARY	1989-90	88	●		●		●		●	●
B	CUSTOM BLACK BEAUTY 54	1992-current	81	●		●		●		●	●
B	CUSTOM BLACK BEAUTY 57 (2 pickups)	1992-current	81	●		●		●		●	●
B	CUSTOM BLACK BEAUTY 57 (3 pickups)	1992-current	81	●		●		●		●	●
B	CUSTOM PLUS	1992-current	81	●		●		●		●	●
B	CUSTOM PREMIUM PLUS	1993-current	81	●		●				●	●
S	25/50 ANNIVERSARY	1978-79	88	●		●		●		●	●
S	CUSTOM/400	1992-current	81	●		●		●		●	●
A	ARTISAN 1st version (three pickups)	1977-79	80	●		●		●		●	●
A	ARTISAN 2nd version (two pickups)	1978-82	80	●		●		●		●	●

	PICKUPS											BRIDGE							HARDWARE		
ONE PICKUP	TWO PICKUPS	THREE PICKUPS	METAL-COVER HUMBUCKER	PLAIN-COVER HUMBUCKER	COVERLESS HUMBUCKER	PLASTIC COVER SINGLE-COIL	MINI METAL-COVER HUMBUCKER	LOW IMPEDANCE: ROUND END	LOW IMPEDANCE: RECTANGULAR	NO PICKGUARD	TRAPEZE BRIDGE/TAILPIECE	WRAPOVER BRIDGE/TAILPIECE	6-SADDLE BRIDGE + BAR TAILPIECE	6-SADDLE BRIDGE + FINE TUNE TAILPIECE	6-SADDLE BRIDGE + VIBRATO TAILPIECE	4-SADDLE BRIDGE/TAILPIECE	ACOUSTIC-STYLE BRIDGE	CHROME/ NICKEL-PLATED	GOLD-PLATED	BLACK-PLATED
	●		●										●						●	
	●		●										●		○			●		
	●		●	●						●			●		○				○	●
	●		●			●							●						●	
○	●	●											●						●	
	●	○	●										●				○		●	
	●		●				●						●					●		
	●					●							●						●	
	●		●										●						●	
	●		●										●						●	
	●						●						●					●		
	●		●											●					●	
	●		●										●		○				●	○
		●	●										●						●	
	●					●							●						●	
	●		●										●						●	
		●	●										●						●	
	●		●						●				●						●	
	●		●						●										●	
	●		●											●				✴	✴	
	●		●										●						●	
		●	●										●	○					●	
	●		●											●					●	

SG SHAPE

This was a complete re-design of the Les Paul, introduced in 1961. The body shape was more adventurous, featuring bevelled edges and twin cutaways, and the result was lighter than the basic Les Paul shape that it replaced. Early examples retained the Les Paul name, but the range was quickly renamed 'SG' and is still in production today.

○ Available at some periods. See page reference for more information.

		PRODUCTION PERIOD	PAGE REFERENCE	FINGERBOARD				HEADSTOCK		BODY	
				BOUND FINGERBOARD	ROSEWOOD	EBONY	MAPLE	METAL TUNER BUTTONS	PLASTIC TUNER BUTTONS	BOUND BODY	CARVED TOP
C	'SG/LES PAUL' STANDARD	1961-63	85	●	●				●		
D	'SG/LES PAUL' JUNIOR	1961-63	85		●				●		
B	'SG/LES PAUL' CUSTOM	1961-63	85	●		●		●			
B	'SG/LES PAUL' CUSTOM re-issue	1987-90	85	●		●		●			
B	'SG/LES PAUL' CUSTOM 30th ANNIVERSARY	1991-92	88	●		●					

SINGLE-CUT SHAPE

This is the single-cutaway design used for the first Junior, TV and Special models, launched by Gibson in 1954 and 1955. It is inspired by the basic Les Paul shape, but at the time was clearly differentiated by virtue of its flat, uncarved-top, in contrast to the carved-top of the existing Les Paul models of the mid-1950s.

		PRODUCTION PERIOD	PAGE REFERENCE	BOUND FINGERBOARD	ROSEWOOD	EBONY	MAPLE	METAL TUNER BUTTONS	PLASTIC TUNER BUTTONS	BOUND BODY	CARVED TOP
D	JUNIOR 'SINGLE-CUT'	1954-58	83		●				●		
D	TV 'SINGLE-CUT'	1955-58	88		●				●		
D	SPECIAL 'SINGLE-CUT'	1955-58	86	●	●				●		
D	JUNIOR 'SINGLE-CUT THREE-QUARTER'	1956-58	83		●				●		
D	SPECIAL 55 (single-cut)	1974, 77-80	86		●			●	○		
D	JUNIOR 54 (single-cut)	1986-91	83		●				●		
D	SPECIAL 'SINGLE-CUT' re-issue ('Junior 11')	1988-current	87	●	●				●		

FINGERBOARD MARKERS

Position indicators come in a variety of shapes on these Les Paul models.

C CROWN   D DOT   B BLOCK

	ONE PICKUP	TWO PICKUPS	THREE PICKUPS	METAL-COVER HUMBUCKER	PLAIN-COVER HUMBUCKER	COVERLESS HUMBUCKER	PLASTIC COVER SINGLE-COIL	MINI METAL-COVER HUMBUCKER	LOW IMPEDANCE: ROUND END	LOW IMPEDANCE: RECTANGULAR	NO PICKGUARD	TRAPEZE BRIDGE/TAILPIECE	WRAPOVER BRIDGE/TAILPIECE	6-SADDLE BRIDGE + BAR TAILPIECE	6-SADDLE BRIDGE + FINE TUNE TAILPIECE	6-SADDLE BRIDGE + VIBRATO TAILPIECE	4-SADDLE BRIDGE/TAILPIECE	ACOUSTIC-STYLE BRIDGE	CHROME-/NICKEL-PLATED	GOLD-PLATED	BLACK-PLATED
		●		●											●				●		
	●						●					●			○				●		
			●	●											●					●	
			●	●									●							●	
			●	●									●							●	

FINGERBOARD MARKERS

Position indicators come in one shape on these Les Paul models.

D DOT

	ONE PICKUP	TWO PICKUPS	THREE PICKUPS	METAL-COVER HUMBUCKER	PLAIN-COVER HUMBUCKER	COVERLESS HUMBUCKER	PLASTIC COVER SINGLE-COIL	MINI METAL-COVER HUMBUCKER	LOW IMPEDANCE: ROUND END	LOW IMPEDANCE: RECTANGULAR	NO PICKGUARD	TRAPEZE BRIDGE/TAILPIECE	WRAPOVER BRIDGE/TAILPIECE	6-SADDLE BRIDGE + BAR TAILPIECE	6-SADDLE BRIDGE + FINE TUNE TAILPIECE	6-SADDLE BRIDGE + VIBRATO TAILPIECE	4-SADDLE BRIDGE/TAILPIECE	ACOUSTIC-STYLE BRIDGE	CHROME-/NICKEL-PLATED	GOLD-PLATED	BLACK-PLATED
	●						●						●						●		
	●						●						●						●		
		○					●						●						●		
	●						●						●						●		
		●					●					○	●						●		
	●						●						●						●		
		●					●						●						●		

DOUBLE-CUT SHAPE

In 1958 and 1959 Gibson radically altered the shape of the Junior, TV and Special models with the introduction of this double-cutaway design. The company were responding to musicians' demands for guitars with an extra cutaway for easier access to the upper frets, and also used the idea on the ES335 semi-acoustic model introduced at the same time.

○ Available at some periods. See page reference for more information.

	Production Period	Page Reference	Bound Fingerboard	Rosewood	FINGERBOARD		HEADSTOCK		BODY	
					Ebony	Maple	Metal Tuner Buttons	Plastic Tuner Buttons	Bound Body	Carved Top
D TV 'DOUBLE-CUT'	1958-59	88		●				●		
D JUNIOR 'DOUBLE-CUT'	1958-61	83		●				●		
D JUNIOR 'DOUBLE-CUT THREE-QUARTER'	1958-61	83		●				●		
D SPECIAL 'DOUBLE-CUT'	1959	86	●	●				●		
D SPECIAL 'DOUBLE-CUT THREE-QUARTER'	1959	86	●	●				●		
D SPECIAL 58 (double-cut)	1976-79	86		●				●		
D JUNIOR 58 (double-cut)	1986-87	83		●				●		

SIGNATURE SHAPE

This is a rather uncomfortable marriage of two Gibson styles. The design appears to have one ES-shape cutaway and one Les Paul-shape cutaway. A broad strip of binding down the tip of the Les Paul cutaway indicates that this shape was not easy to produce on a hollow-body guitar, and the design did not last long in the Gibson catalog.

	Production Period	Page Reference	Bound Fingerboard	Rosewood	Ebony	Maple	Metal Tuner Buttons	Plastic Tuner Buttons	Bound Body	Carved Top
C SIGNATURE	1974-78	86	●	●				●	●	
C SIGNATURE BASS	1974-79	86		●			●		●	

PROFESSIONAL/PERSONAL SHAPE

The Professional and Personal models heralded the beginning of an experiment by Gibson using low impedance pickups. The two models used a design virtually identical to the basic Les Paul shape, but about half-an-inch bigger all the way around the outline. The extra weight of the guitars did not help their general unpopularity.

	Production Period	Page Reference	Bound Fingerboard	Rosewood	Ebony	Maple	Metal Tuner Buttons	Plastic Tuner Buttons	Bound Body	Carved Top
C PROFESSIONAL	1969-71	85	●	●				●	●	●
B PERSONAL	1969-72	84	●		●			●	●	●

FINGERBOARD MARKERS

Position indicators come in one shape on these Les Paul models.

D DOT

	PICKUPS											BRIDGE							HARDWARE		
ONE PICKUP	TWO PICKUPS	THREE PICKUPS	METAL-COVER HUMBUCKER	PLAIN-COVER HUMBUCKER	COVERLESS HUMBUCKER	PLASTIC COVER SINGLE-COIL	MINI METAL-COVER HUMBUCKER	LOW IMPEDANCE: ROUND END	LOW IMPEDANCE: RECTANGULAR	NO PICKGUARD	TRAPEZE BRIDGE/TAILPIECE	WRAPOVER BRIDGE/TAILPIECE	6-SADDLE BRIDGE + BAR TAILPIECE	6-SADDLE BRIDGE + FINE TUNE TAILPIECE	6-SADDLE BRIDGE + VIBRATO TAILPIECE	4-SADDLE BRIDGE/TAILPIECE	ACOUSTIC-STYLE BRIDGE	CHROME-/NICKEL-PLATED	GOLD-PLATED	BLACK-PLATED
•						•						•						•		
•						•						•						•		
•						•						•						•		
	•					•						•						•		
	•					•						•						•		
	•					•							•					•		
•						•							•					•		

FINGERBOARD MARKERS

Position indicators come in one shape on these Les Paul models.

C CROWN

FINGERBOARD MARKERS

Position indicators come in two shapes on these Les Paul models.

C CROWN   **B BLOCK**

1970s BASS SHAPE

Again, this was clearly a derivative of the basic Les Paul shape, introduced for the first bass guitar to bear the name. The Les Paul Bass and Triumph Bass followed the Professional and Personal models in using low impedance pickups, and like many of Gibson's bass guitars did not enjoy wide appeal.

○ Available at some periods. See page reference for more information.

		PRODUCTION PERIOD	PAGE REFERENCE	BOUND FINGERBOARD	FINGERBOARD			HEADSTOCK		BODY	
					ROSEWOOD	EBONY	MAPLE	METAL TUNER BUTTONS	PLASTIC TUNER BUTTONS	BOUND BODY	CARVED TOP
D	BASS 1st version (most controls not on panel)	1969-70	83		●			●		●	●
B	TRIUMPH BASS (BASS 2nd version: all controls on panel)	1971-79	83	●	●			●		●	●

1990s BASS SHAPE

In 1992 Gibson re-introduced the idea of a Les Paul bass guitar, and once again used the basic Les Paul shape as the inspiration for the design. There were a number of models in the new series, using established Gibson Les Paul names such as Deluxe, Standard and Special.

		PRODUCTION PERIOD	PAGE REFERENCE	BOUND FINGERBOARD	ROSEWOOD	EBONY	MAPLE	METAL TUNER BUTTONS	PLASTIC TUNER BUTTONS	BOUND BODY	CARVED TOP
C	DELUXE BASS LPB2	1992-current	84			●		●		●	
C	STANDARD BASS LPB3	1992-current	84			●		●		●	●
C	DELUXE PLUS BASS	1993-current	84			●		●		●	
C	DELUXE PREMIUM PLUS BASS	1993-current	84			●		●		●	
C	STANDARD PLUS BASS	1993-current	84			●		●		●	●
C	STANDARD PREMIUM PLUS BASS	1993-current	84			●		●		●	●
D	SPECIAL BASS LPB1	1992-current	84			●		●			

ACOUSTIC BODY SHAPE

Something of an oddball among the Gibson models which have appeared with the Les Paul name over the years is the Jumbo, a shortlived guitar that was only in production around 1970. It used a traditional flat-top body, combined with Gibson's hot idea of the moment, a low impedance pickup.

		PRODUCTION PERIOD	PAGE REFERENCE	BOUND FINGERBOARD	ROSEWOOD	EBONY	MAPLE	METAL TUNER BUTTONS	PLASTIC TUNER BUTTONS	BOUND BODY	CARVED TOP
D	JUMBO	1970-71	83		●			●		●	

FINGERBOARD MARKERS
Position indicators come in two shapes on these Les Paul models.

D DOT   **B** BLOCK

Column headers

PICKUPS: ONE PICKUP | TWO PICKUPS | THREE PICKUPS | METAL-COVER HUMBUCKER | PLAIN-COVER HUMBUCKER | COVERLESS HUMBUCKER | PLASTIC COVER SINGLE-COIL | MINI METAL-COVER HUMBUCKER | LOW IMPEDANCE: ROUND END | LOW IMPEDANCE: RECTANGULAR

NO PICKGUARD

BRIDGE: TRAPEZE BRIDGE/TAILPIECE | WRAPOVER BRIDGE/TAILPIECE | 6-SADDLE BRIDGE + BAR TAILPIECE | 6-SADDLE BRIDGE + FINE TUNE TAILPIECE | 6-SADDLE BRIDGE + VIBRATO TAILPIECE | 4-SADDLE BRIDGE/TAILPIECE | ACOUSTIC-STYLE BRIDGE

HARDWARE: CHROME/NICKEL-PLATED | GOLD-PLATED | BLACK-PLATED

Two Pickups	Low Imp. Round End	No Pickguard	4-Saddle Bridge/Tailpiece	Chrome/Nickel-Plated
●	●	●	●	●
●	●	●	●	●

FINGERBOARD MARKERS
Position indicators come in two shapes on these Les Paul models.

C CROWN   **D** DOT

Pickups	No Pickguard	Bridge	Hardware
Two Pickups, Plain-Cover Humbucker	●	6-Saddle Fine Tune	Black-Plated
Two Pickups, Three Pickups	●	6-Saddle Fine Tune	Gold-Plated
Two Pickups, Plain-Cover Humbucker	●	6-Saddle Fine Tune	Black-Plated
Two Pickups, Plain-Cover Humbucker	●	6-Saddle Fine Tune	Black-Plated
Two Pickups, Three Pickups	●	6-Saddle Fine Tune	Chrome/Nickel
Two Pickups, Plain-Cover Humbucker	●	6-Saddle Fine Tune	—
Two Pickups, Plain-Cover Humbucker	●	6-Saddle Fine Tune	—

FINGERBOARD MARKERS
Position indicators come in one shape on this Les Paul model.

D DOT

One Pickup	Plain-Cover Humbucker	No Pickguard	4-Saddle	Chrome/Nickel
●	●		●	●

The main Reference Listing (pages 80-88) uses a simple, condensed format to convey a large amount of information about every Gibson Les Paul model, and the following notes are intended to ensure that you gain the most from this unique inventory.

Individual entries in the Reference Listing contain all or some of the following:

MODEL NAME; DATE OR RANGE OF DATES IN PRODUCTION; BRIEF ONE-SENTENCE IDENTIFICATION; REFERENCE TO ANOTHER MODEL ENTRY; LIST OF SPECIFICATION POINTS; VARIATIONS; GENERAL COMMENTS; GIBSON SHIPPING TOTALS.

We'll explain each of these in more detail. At the head of each entry is the MODEL NAME in bold type, listed in alphabetical order. This is followed by a DATE OR RANGE OF DATES showing the production period of the instrument. These dates, and any other dates shown in the Reference Section, are approximate. In many cases it is virtually impossible to pinpoint with total accuracy the period during which a model was in production at the factory.

Gibson's promotional catalogues usually bear dates, but the content was often decided far in advance and does not always reflect what was being made when the catalogue was eventually issued. Similarly, Gibson's dated pricelists itemize the models that the company were selling at any one time, and not necessarily the guitars that were then in production.

Gibson's lists of the numbers of guitars 'shipped' (ie leaving the factory) sometimes show guitars made in years beyond the range we give for production. We assume that where only a small quantity of guitars is shown for a model otherwise produced in reasonably substantial numbers, these are either samples (made before the start of a production period) or leftovers being sold off (after production has ceased).

Naturally we have gone to some lengths to list the most accurate dates possible for the production periods and changes made to Gibson's Les Paul models. But please treat them as approximate, because that is all they can be.

In italics, following the model name and production dates, is a BRIEF ONE-SENTENCE IDENTIFICATION of the guitar in question. This is intended to help you recognize a specific model at a glance. To enable you to do this we have noted elements of the guitar's design that are unique to that particular model.

For some guitars there may be a sentence below this, reading 'Similar to . . . except:' or 'As . . . except:'. This will take the form of a REFERENCE TO ANOTHER MODEL ENTRY. The description will list any major differences between the two models.

The LIST OF SPECIFICATION POINTS, separated into groups, provides details of the model's features. In the order listed the points refer to:

- Neck, fingerboard, headstock.
- Body.
- Pickups.
- Controls.
- Pickguard.
- Bridge*.
- Hardware finish.

Note that Bigsby vibrato tailpieces were and are available as an option on many models, but that this option is not recorded in the Reference Listing.

Of course, not every model will need all seven points. And to avoid repetition in the specification points, we have considered a number of features to be common to all Gibson Les Paul models. They are:

Plastic truss-rod cover unless stated.

Metal tuner buttons unless stated.

22 frets unless stated.

Scale length approximately 24.6in unless stated.

Single-cutaway body unless stated.

Side-mounted jack socket unless stated.

Nickel- or chrome-plated hardware unless stated.

Some models were made in a number of VARIATIONS, and where applicable these are listed after the specification points, in italics. Any other GENERAL COMMENTS are also made in this position.

At the end of each entry or group of entries, sometimes we show GIBSON SHIPPING TOTALS. These are taken from official Gibson records showing the number of guitars shipped from (ie leaving) the Kalamazoo factory each year. These were totalled each month by Shipping Department staff and subsequently entered onto a yearly report. These figures shown in the Reference Listing should be treated with caution: the calculations were tallied by hand, and human error is very evident. The figures we've used here continue to 1979, but we could find no figures for Kalamazoo from 1980 to its closure in 1984, and no figures for any Nashville production from its opening in 1975 until the late 1980s – these are apparently lost in a computer file somewhere. Figures are being kept again by the new owners, but for commercial reasons they will not release them.

All this information is designed to tell you more about your Gibson Les Paul guitar. By using the general information and illustrations earlier in the book combined with the knowledge obtained from the reference section you should be able to build up a very full picture of your instrument and its pedigree.

GIBSON LES PAUL REFERENCE LISTING:
ALL MODELS 1952-1993

80

ARTISAN

'FIRST VERSION' 1977-79 *Ornate fingerboard markers, three pickups.*
■ Bound ebony fingerboard, ornate markers; script Gibson logo and ornate inlay on headstock; 'Artisan' on truss-rod cover.
■ Bound carved-top body; sunburst, brown or black.
■ Three metal-cover humbucker pickups.
■ Four controls (two volume, two tone) plus three-way selector.
■ Black laminated plastic pickguard.
■ Six-saddle bridge plus separate bar tailpiece.
■ Gold-plated hardware.
Some examples with separate bar tailpiece with six fine-tuning knobs.

'SECOND VERSION' 1978-82 *Ornate fingerboard markers, two pickups.*
Similar to 'FIRST VERSION' except:
■ Two metal-cover humbucker pickups.
■ Six-saddle bridge plus separate bar tailpiece with six fine-tuning knobs.

GIBSON SHIPPING TOTALS for Artisan models: **1976** 2; **1977** 1469; **1978** 641; **1979** 108. Figures not available for 1980s.

ARTIST

1979-81 *Block fingerboard markers, 'LP' headstock inlay, three controls and three mini-switches.*
■ Bound ebony fingerboard, block markers; 'LP' inlay on headstock; metal truss-rod cover; brass nut.
■ Bound carved-top body; sunbursts or black.

■ Two metal-cover humbucker pickups.
■ Three controls (volume, bass, treble) plus three-way selector, three mini-switches; active circuit.
■ Black laminated plastic pickguard.
■ Six-saddle bridge plus separate bar tailpiece with six fine-tuning knobs.
■ Gold-plated hardware.

GIBSON SHIPPING TOTAL for Artist model: **1979** 234. Figures not available for 1980 and 1981.

'BLACK BEAUTY'

See later CUSTOM entry.

CLASSIC

CLASSIC 1990-current *'Classic' on truss-rod cover.*
■ Bound rosewood fingerboard, crown markers; 'Les Paul Model' on headstock; 'Classic' on truss-rod cover; plastic tuner buttons.
■ Bound carved-top body; sunbursts or colors.
■ Two coverless humbuckers.
■ Four controls (two volume, two tone) plus three-way selector.
■ Cream plastic pickguard with '1960' logo.
■ Six-saddle bridge plus separate bar tailpiece.

CLASSIC CELEBRITY 1992 *'Celebrity' on pickguard.*
Similar to CLASSIC, except:
■ Bound ebony fingerboard.
■ Black only.

■ White plastic pickguard with 'Celebrity' logo.
■ Gold-plated hardware.
Limited run of 200 units.

CLASSIC/MIII 1991-92 *Additional central single-coil pickup; bound fingerboard.*
Similar to CLASSIC, except:
■ Sunburst only.
■ Two coverless humbuckers plus one central six-polepiece single-coil pickup.
■ Two controls (volume, tone) plus five-way selector and mini-switch.
■ No pickguard.

CLASSIC PLUS 1992-current
CLASSIC PREMIUM PLUS 1993-current
CLASSIC BIRDSEYE 1993-current
CLASSIC PREMIUM BIRDSEYE 1993-current
All similar to CLASSIC, except:
■ Varying grades of figured maple carved-top (Premium Plus better than Plus, Premium Birdseye better than Birdseye).

CUSTOM

NORMAL MODELS chronological order

'FIRST VERSION' 1954-57 *Block fingerboard markers, split-diamond headstock inlay, 'Les Paul Custom' on truss-rod cover, two plastic-cover pickups.*
■ Bound ebony fingerboard, block markers; split-diamond inlay on headstock; 'Les Paul Custom' on truss-rod cover.
■ Bound carved-top body; black only.
■ Two plastic-cover six-polepiece single-coil pickups (neck unit with oblong polepieces; bridge unit with round polepieces).

■ Four controls (two volume, two tone) plus three-way selector.
■ Black laminated plastic pickguard.
■ Six-saddle bridge plus separate bar tailpiece.
■ Gold-plated hardware.

'SECOND VERSION' 1957-61 *Humbucker pickups.*
Similar to 'FIRST VERSION', except:
■ Three metal-cover humbucker pickups.
Some with two humbucker pickups.
Shape changed in 1961: see later 'SG/ LES PAUL' CUSTOM entry.
Also 35th Anniversary version with appropriate inlay on headstock (1989-90): see later 35th ANNIVERSARY entry.

'THIRD VERSION' 1968-current *Two humbuckers.*
Similar to 'SECOND VERSION', except:
■ Sunbursts, natural or colors.
■ Two metal-cover humbucker pickups.
Also three-humbucker version (various periods during 1970s, 1980s & 1990s).
Also versions with nickel-plated hardware (1976-83) or chrome-plated hardware (1983-87).
Also maple fingerboard version (1976-80).
Also 20th Anniversary version with appropriate inlay at 15th fret (1974): see later 20th ANNIVERSARY entry.

GIBSON SHIPPING TOTALS for Custom models made at Kalamazoo: **1954** 94; **1955** 355; **1956** 489; **1957** 283; **1958** 256; **1959** 246; **1960** 189; **1961** 513 (includes some 'SG/Les' Custom models); **1968** 433; **1969** 2353; **1970** 2612; **1971** 3201; **1972** 4002; **1973** 7232; **1974** 7563; **1975** 7448; **1976** 4323; **1977** 3133; **1978** 10,744; **1979** 1624. Figures not available for large Nashville production started 1975, nor for 1980s & 1990s.

OTHER CUSTOM MODELS alphabetical order

BLACK BEAUTY 54 1992-current *Re-issue based on 'FIRST VERSION' but bridge pickup, although visually similar, is actually a humbucker.*

BLACK BEAUTY 57 1992-current *Re-issue based on rare two-humbucker 'SECOND VERSION'.*

BLACK BEAUTY 57 3-PICKUP 1992-current *Re-issue based on 'SECOND VERSION'. Also 35th Anniversary version with appropriate inlay on headstock (1989-90): see later 35th ANNIVERSARY entry.*

CUSTOM PLUS 1992-current
CUSTOM PREMIUM PLUS 1993-current
Both similar to 'THIRD VERSION', except:
■ Varying grades of figured maple carved-top (Premium Plus is better than Plus); sunbursts.
■ No pickguard.

CUSTOM/400 1992-current *Split-block fingerboard markers, Custom Shop Edition logo on rear of headstock.*
Similar to 'THIRD VERSION', except:
■ Bound ebony fingerboard, split-block markers; 'Custom Shop Edition' logo on rear of headstock.
■ Bound carved-top body; black only.
■ Gold-plated hardware.
Name derives from Custom-style appointments and Gibson Super 400-style fingerboard markers.

'54 LTD EDITION' 1972-73 *Re-issue based on 'FIRST VERSION', identifiable by serial number prefixed with LE.*

GIBSON SHIPPING TOTALS for Custom '54 Ltd Edition' models: **1972** 60; **1973** 1090; **1975** 3; **1977** 1.

CUSTOM LITE

1987-89 *Contoured, thinner body; block fingerboard markers.*
■ Bound ebony fingerboard, block markers; split-diamond inlay on headstock.
■ Bound carved-top thinner body with contoured back; sunburst, black or pink.
■ Two metal-cover humbucker pickups.

■ Three controls (two volumes, one tone) plus three-way selector (two controls plus three-way selector 1989) and mini-switch.
■ Black laminated plastic pickguard.
■ Six-saddle bridge plus separate bar tailpiece. Six-saddle locking bridge/ vibrato unit option.
■ Gold-plated hardware (black-plated 1989).

CUSTOM SHOP

Special one-off custom orders were available from Gibson's original factory in Kalamazoo from its earliest days, but a bona fide Custom Department wasn't officially established until the 1960s. There was a Custom Shop at the current Nashville factory from 1983 until 1988, and then again from 1992 effectively as two operations: one, building artists' guitars, is coupled with R&D; the other is dedicated to producing custom orders for dealers. The Custom Shop's purpose has been and is to manufacture special models, custom-order one-offs and limited edition production runs in relatively small quantities. These have included exclusive guitars for dealers such as Guitar Trader, Leo's, Jimmy Wallace, Norman's Rare Guitars and others. Some Custom Shop instruments have been elaborate versions of stock items, employing higher quality timbers, better hardware, or impressive finishes – for example the recent models extravagantly inlaid with pearl by Greg Rich. Custom Shop guitars sometimes carry an identifying logo on the back of the headstock. (See also listings for SPOTLIGHT SPECIAL and CUSTOM/400 models).

81

DELUXE

1969-84 'Deluxe' on truss-rod cover.
- Bound rosewood fingerboard, crown markers; 'Les Paul Model' on headstock; 'Deluxe' on truss-rod cover; plastic tuner buttons (later metal).
- Bound carved-top body; sunbursts, natural or colors.
- Two mini-sized metal-cover humbucker pickups.
- Four controls (two volume, two tone) plus three-way selector.
- Cream plastic pickguard.
- Six-saddle bridge plus separate bar tailpiece.

Earliest examples with plastic-cover six-polepiece single-coil pickups.
Some mini-humbucker-equipped examples with extra plastic ring around pickup covers.
Also some examples with normal-sized humbuckers.

GIBSON SHIPPING TOTALS for Deluxe models made at Kalamazoo: **1971** 4466; **1972** 5194; **1973** 10,484; **1974** 7367; **1975** 2561; **1976** 172; **1977** 413; **1978** 4450; **1979** 413. Figures not available for 1969, 1970s and 1980s, nor for any Nashville production.

'RE-ISSUE' 1992-current *Re-issue based on original version.*

DOUBLE CUTAWAY XPL

This model is beyond our coverage since the guitar does not bear the Les Paul name (despite references to the contrary in Gibson literature).

EPIPHONE

Gibson acquired the Epiphone brandname in 1957 and started making Epiphone guitars in 1959. They ceased all production of Epiphone in the USA in 1970, having started around 1968 to transfer the brandname to instruments made in Japan. In the late 1980s these were succeeded by Epiphone models made in Korea. Regardless of origin, at the time of writing only one Epiphone has carried the Les Paul logo, this being the Korean-built LES PAUL STANDARD, introduced in 1988 and still in production.

'GOLD-TOP'

'FIRST VERSION' 1952-53 *Crown fingerboard markers, two plastic-cover pickups, bridge/tailpiece on long 'trapeze' anchor.*
- Bound rosewood fingerboard, crown markers; 'Les Paul Model' on headstock; plastic tuner buttons.
- Bound carved-top body; gold only.
- Two plastic-cover six-polepiece single-coil pickups.
- Four controls (two volume, two tone) plus three-way selector.
- Cream plastic pickguard.
- Wrap-under bar bridge/tailpiece on long 'trapeze' anchor.

Some early examples do not have a bound fingerboard.
Most examples do not have a serial number.
Some with all-gold body (rather than normal gold top with brown back and sides).

'SECOND VERSION' 1953-55 *Angled one-piece bridge/tailpiece.*
Similar to 'FIRST VERSION', except:
- Wrap-over bar bridge/tailpiece.
Some with all-gold body.

'THIRD VERSION' 1955-57 *Six-saddle bridge plus separate bar tailpiece, two plastic-cover pickups.*

Similar to 'SECOND VERSION', except:
- Six-saddle bridge plus separate bar tailpiece.

'FOURTH VERSION' 1957-58 *Two humbuckers, six-saddle bridge plus separate bar tailpiece.*
Similar to 'THIRD VERSION', except:
- Two metal-cover humbucker pickups.
Finish changed to sunburst in 1958: see later 'SUNBURST' entry.

'FIFTH VERSION' 1968-69 *Based on 'THIRD VERSION' (bridge and separate tailpiece), but wide binding in cutaway. Confusingly referred to in Gibson literature as 'Standard' model.*

'SIXTH VERSION' 1971-72 *Based on 'SECOND VERSION' (one-piece bridge/tailpiece), but with Gibson logo on pickups. Some examples with extra plastic ring around pickup covers.*

'57 RE-ISSUE' 1985-current *Based on 'FOURTH VERSION' (metal-cover humbuckers; bridge and separate tailpiece).*

'56 RE-ISSUE' 1989-current *Based on 'THIRD VERSION' (plastic-cover pickups; bridge and separate tailpiece), but pickups, although visually similar, are actually humbucking types.*

GIBSON SHIPPING TOTALS for 'Gold-top' models: **1952** 1716; **1953** 2245; **1954** 1504; **1955** 862; **1956** 920; **1957** 598; **1958** 434 (includes some 'Sunburst' models); **1968** 1224; **1969** 2751; **1971** 25; **1972** 1046; **1973** 4; **1974** 1. Figures not available for 1980s & 1990s.

HERITAGE SERIES

STANDARD 80 1980-82 *'Heritage Series Standard-80' on truss-rod cover; extra four-figure number on back of headstock.*
- Bound rosewood fingerboard, crown markers; 'Les Paul Model' on headstock; 'Heritage Series Standard-80' on truss-rod cover; four-

figure number on back of headstock in addition to normal serial number.
■ Bound carved-top body; sunbursts.
■ Two metal-cover humbucker pickups.
■ Four controls (two volume, two tone) plus three-way selector.
■ Cream plastic pickguard.
■ Six-saddle bridge plus separate bar tailpiece.

STANDARD 80 ELITE 1980-82 *'Heritage Series Standard-80 Elite' on truss-rod cover; additional four-figure serial number on back of headstock.*
Similar to STANDARD 80, except:
■ Bound ebony fingerboard; 'Heritage Series Standard-80 Elite' on truss-rod cover.
■ Quilted maple carved-top.

JUMBO

1970-71 *Round soundhole.*
■ Rosewood fingerboard, dot markers; 'Les Paul Jumbo' on truss-rod cover.
■ Bound single-cutaway Jumbo acoustic body; natural.
■ One round-end plastic-cover low-impedance humbucker pickup.
■ Four controls (volume, treble, bass, 'Decade') plus bypass switch.
■ Black plastic pickguard.
■ Height-adjustable one-piece bridge with string-anchor pins in wooden surround.
Requires special cord with built-in impedance-matching transformer to match normal amplification impedance.

GIBSON SHIPPING TOTALS for Jumbo models: **1971** 43; **1972** 3; **1973** 3. Figures not available for 1970.

JUNIOR

NORMAL MODELS chronological order

'SINGLE-CUT' 1954-58 *Slab single-cutaway body, one pickup.*
■ Unbound rosewood fingerboard, dot markers; 'Les Paul Junior' on headstock; plastic tuner buttons.

■ Unbound slab body; sunburst. (For beige examples, see later TV entry.)
■ One plastic-cover six-polepiece single-coil pickup.
■ Two controls (volume, tone).
■ Black or tortoiseshell plastic pickguard.
■ Wrap-over bar bridge/tailpiece.

'SINGLE-CUT THREE-QUARTER' 1956-58 *Shorter 19-fret neck.*
Similar to 'SINGLE-CUT' except:
■ Shorter neck (with 19 frets) and scale-length (2in less than normal).

'DOUBLE-CUT' 1958-61 *Slab double-cutaway body, one pickup.*
■ Unbound rosewood fingerboard, dot markers; 'Les Paul Junior' on headstock; plastic tuner buttons.
■ Unbound slab double-cutaway body; cherry. (For yellow examples, see later TV entry.)
■ One plastic-cover six-polepiece single-coil pickup.
■ Two controls (volume, tone).
■ Black or tortoiseshell plastic pickguard.
■ Wrap-over bar bridge/tailpiece.
Shape changed in 1961: see later 'SG/ LES PAUL' JUNIOR entry.
Some examples in sunburst.

'DOUBLE-CUT THREE-QUARTER' 1958-61 *Shorter 19-fret neck.*
Similar to 'DOUBLE-CUT' except:
■ Shorter neck (with 19 frets) and scale-length (2in less than normal).

GIBSON SHIPPING TOTALS for Junior models: **1954** 823; **1955** 2839; **1956** 3129; **1957** 2959; **1958** 2408; **1959** 4364; **1960** 2513; **1961** 2151 (includes some 'SG/Les Paul' Junior models). And for Junior ³/₄ models: **1956** 18; **1957** 222; **1958** 181; **1959** 199; **1960** 96; **1961** 71.

OTHER JUNIOR MODELS alphabetical order

'JUNIOR II' see SPECIAL 'SINGLE-CUT RE-ISSUE' in later SPECIAL entry.

'54' 1986-91 *Based on 'SINGLE-CUT' but six-saddle bridge plus separate bar tailpiece; sunburst, cherry or white.*

'58' 1986-87 *Based on 'DOUBLE-CUT' but six-saddle bridge plus separate bar tailpiece.*

KM

1979 *'Les Paul K.M.' on truss-rod cover.*
■ Bound rosewood fingerboard, crown markers; 'Les Paul K.M.' on truss-rod cover.
■ Bound carved-top body; sunbursts or natural.
■ Two coverless humbucker pickups.
■ Four controls (two volume, two tone) plus three-way selector.
■ Cream plastic pickguard.
■ Six-saddle bridge plus separate bar tailpiece.
Some with 'Custom Made' plastic plate on body face.

GIBSON SHIPPING TOTAL for KM model: **1979** 1052.

LES PAUL BASS

'FIRST VERSION' 1969-70 *24 frets, dot markers, most controls not on panel.*
■ Unbound rosewood fingerboard, dot markers; 24 frets, 30.5in scale-length; crown inlay on headstock.
■ Bound carved-top body; brown.
■ Two round-end plastic-cover low-impedance humbucker pickups.
■ Three controls (volume, bass, treble) plus three-way selector, all on body; phase slide switch and tone selector on small panel.
■ No pickguard.
■ Four-saddle bridge/tailpiece with integral damper; plus metal cover.
Requires special cord with built-in impedance-matching transformer to match normal amplification impedance.

'SECOND VERSION' (also known as **LES PAUL TRIUMPH BASS**) 1971-79 *24 frets, block markers, all controls on panel.*
■ Bound rosewood fingerboard, block markers; 24 frets, 30.5in scale-length; split-diamond inlay on headstock.

83

■ Bound carved-top body; brown or white.
■ Two round-end plastic-cover low-impedance humbucker pickups.
■ Three controls (volume, bass, treble) plus three-way selector, phase slide switch, tone selector, impedance slide switch, and jack socket, all on black laminated plastic panel; built-in impedance-matching transformer.
■ No pickguard.
■ Four-saddle bridge/tailpiece; plus metal cover.

GIBSON SHIPPING TOTALS for Bass and/or Triumph Bass models: **1971** 321; **1972** 768; **1973** 959; **1974** 526; **1975** 208; **1976** 171; **1977** 101; **1978** 80; **1979** 44. Figures not available for 1969 and 1970.

LES PAUL BASSES – '1990s SERIES'

DELUXE BASS 1992-current *20 frets, crown markers, black-plated hardware.*
■ Unbound ebony fingerboard, crown markers; 20 frets, 34in scale-length; ornate 'flower pot' inlay on headstock (omitted from 1993); 'Les Paul' on truss-rod cover.
■ Bound slab body; various colors.
■ Two plain-cover humbucker pickups.
■ Four controls (volume, bass, treble, balance); active circuit.
■ No pickguard.
■ Four-saddle bridge/tailpiece.
■ Black-plated hardware.

DELUXE PLUS BASS 1993-current
DELUXE PREMIUM PLUS BASS 1993-current
Both similar to DELUXE BASS, except:
■ Varying grades of figured maple carved-top (Premium Plus better than Plus).
Also five-string version (1993-current) of Deluxe Premium Plus.

SPECIAL BASS 1992-current *20 frets, dot markers.*
■ Unbound ebony fingerboard, dot markers; 20 frets, 34in scale-length; ornate 'flower pot' inlay on headstock (omitted from 1993); 'Les Paul' on truss-rod cover.

■ Unbound slab body; black, cherry or yellow.
■ Two plain-cover humbucker pickups.
■ 1992 model three controls (volume, volume, tone), passive circuit; from 1993 four controls (volume, bass, treble, balance), active circuit.
■ No pickguard.
■ Four-saddle bridge/tailpiece.
■ Black-plated hardware.
Also five-string version (1993-current).

STANDARD BASS 1992-current *20 frets, crown markers, chrome-plated hardware.*
■ Unbound ebony fingerboard, crown markers; 20 frets, 34in scale-length; ornate 'flower pot' inlay on headstock (omitted from 1993); 'Les Paul' on truss-rod cover.
■ Bound carved-top body; sunbursts or black.
■ Two metal-cover humbucker pickups.
■ 1992 model four controls (two volume, two tone), passive circuit; from 1993 four controls (volume, bass, treble, balance), active circuit.
■ No pickguard.
■ Four-saddle bridge/tailpiece.

STANDARD PLUS BASS 1993-current
STANDARD PREMIUM PLUS BASS 1993-current
Both similar to STANDARD BASS, except:
■ Varying grades of figured maple carved-top (Premium Plus better than Plus).
Also five-string version (1993-current) of Standard Premium Plus.

LP XRI/XRII/XRIII

LP XRI 1981-82 *'XR-I' on truss-rod cover.*
■ Unbound rosewood fingerboard, dot markers; 'Les Paul Model' on headstock; 'XR-I' on truss-rod cover.
■ Unbound carved-top body; sunbursts.
■ Two coverless humbucker pickups.
■ Four controls (two volume, two tone) plus three-way selector and mini-switch.
■ No pickguard.
■ Six-saddle bridge plus separate bar tailpiece.

LP XRII 1981-82 *'XR-II' on truss-rod cover. Similar to LP XRI, except:*
■ 'XR-II' on truss-rod cover.
■ Bound slab body; sunbursts or natural.
■ Two mini-sized metal-cover humbucker pickups.

LP XRIII 1982 *'XR-III' on truss-rod cover.*
■ Possibly red only.
No other information available for this model.

ORVILLE

The first name of the founder of the American company was used by Gibson on a range of Japanese-made guitars, launched in 1988, which officially copy Gibson's most famous designs. While the cheaper guitars carry only the Orville logo, the higher priced versions are branded Orville By Gibson. This latter line bears the 'Les Paul' logo when appropriate, and models include the Custom, Standard and Junior. The Orville By Gibson instruments are equipped with US-made Gibson pickups. At the time of writing these high quality, accurate repros are sold only on the Japanese market, because Gibson does not perceive a market niche for them elsewhere.

PERSONAL

1969-72 Two angled pickups, block markers, gold hardware.
■ Bound ebony fingerboard, block markers; split-diamond inlay on headstock.
■ Bound carved-top body; brown.
■ Two angled round-end plastic-cover low-impedance humbucker pickups.
■ Five controls (volume, bass, treble, Decade, microphone volume) plus three-way selector, all on body; phase slide switch and tone selector on small panel. Microphone input socket on upper left side of body.
■ Black laminated plastic pickguard.

■ Six-saddle bridge plus separate bar tailpiece.
■ Gold-plated hardware.
Requires special cord with built-in impedance-matching transformer to match normal amplification impedance.

GIBSON SHIPPING TOTALS for Personal models: **1971** 95; **1972** 49; **1973** 2. Figures not available for 1969 and 1970.

PRO DELUXE

1976-82 *Bound ebony fingerboard with crown markers.*
■ Bound ebony fingerboard, crown markers; 'Les Paul Model' on headstock; 'Pro' on truss-rod cover.
■ Bound carved-top body; sunbursts or colors.
■ Two plastic-cover six-polepiece single-coil pickups.
■ Four controls (two volume, two tone) plus three-way selector.
■ Cream plastic pickguard.
■ Six-saddle bridge plus separate bar tailpiece.

PROFESSIONAL

1969-71 *Two angled pickups, crown markers, nickel-plated hardware.*
■ Bound rosewood fingerboard, crown markers.
■ Bound carved-top body; brown.
■ Two angled round-end plastic-cover low-impedance humbucker pickups.
■ Four controls (volume, bass, treble, Decade) plus three-way selector, all on body; phase slide switch and tone selector on small panel.
■ Black laminated plastic pickguard.
■ Six-saddle bridge plus separate bar tailpiece.
Requires special cord with built-in impedance-matching transformer to match normal amplification impedance.

GIBSON SHIPPING TOTALS for Professional models: **1971** 116; **1973** 2 **1977** 11; **1978** 1399 (probably a misprint); **1979** 6. Figures not available for 1969 and 1970.

RECORDING

'FIRST VERSION' 1971-77 *'Les Paul Recording' on truss-rod cover; all controls on panel.*
■ Bound rosewood fingerboard, block markers; split-diamond inlay on headstock; 'Les Paul Recording' on truss-rod cover.
■ Bound carved-top body; sunburst, brown or white.
■ Two angled round-end plastic-cover low-impedance humbucker pickups.
■ Four controls (volume, bass, treble, Decade) plus three-way selector, tone selector, phase slide switch, low/high impedance slide switch, and jack socket, all on laminated black plastic panel; built-in impedance-matching transformer.
■ Black laminated plastic pickguard.
■ Six-saddle bridge plus separate bar tailpiece.

'SECOND VERSION' 1977-79 *'Les Paul Recording' on truss-rod cover; selector by neck pickup.*
Similar to 'FIRST VERSION', except:
■ Sunburst, brown, white or black.
■ Bound ebony fingerboard.
■ Four controls (volume, bass, treble, Decade) plus phase slide switch and tone selector, all on laminated black plastic panel; three-way selector on body; one jack socket on side of body for normal high-impedance output, plus second jack socket on body face for low-impedance output.

GIBSON SHIPPING TOTALS for Recording models made at Kalamazoo: **1971** 236; **1972** 1314; **1973** 1759; **1974** 915; **1975** 204; **1976** 352; **1977** 362; **1978** 180; **1979** 78. Figures not available for any Nashville production.

'SG/LES PAUL' CUSTOM

1961-63 *Bevelled-edge two-cutaway body; three pickups.*
■ Bound ebony fingerboard, block markers; split-diamond inlay on headstock; 'Custom' on truss-rod cover.

■ Bevelled-edge two-cutaway body; white only.
■ Three metal-cover humbucker pickups.
■ Four controls (two volume, two tone) plus three-way selector; jack socket on body face.
■ White laminated plastic pickguard, plus small white plastic plate reading 'Les Paul Custom.'
■ Six-saddle bridge plus separate sideways-action vibrato tailpiece.
■ Gold-plated hardware.
Some examples with standard-action vibrato tailpieces, some of which have inlaid decorative block in body face masking holes intended for sideways-action vibrato unit.
Also 30th Anniversary version with appropriate inlay on headstock (1991-92): see later 30th ANNIVERSARY entry.

GIBSON SHIPPING TOTALS for 'SG/Les Paul' Custom models: **1961** 513 (includes some Les Paul Custom models); **1962** 298; **1963** 264 (includes some SG Custom models).

'RE-ISSUE' 1987-90 *Based on original version, but with six-saddle bridge plus separate bar tailpiece.*

'SG/LES PAUL' JUNIOR

1961-63 *Bevelled-edge two-cutaway body; one pickup.*
■ Unbound rosewood fingerboard, dot markers; 'Les Paul Junior' on headstock; plastic tuner buttons.
■ Bevelled-edge two-cutaway body; cherry.
■ One plastic-cover six-polepiece single-coil pickup.
■ Two controls (volume, tone); jack socket on body face.
■ Black laminated plastic pickguard.
■ Wrap-over bar bridge/tailpiece; optional separate vibrato tailpiece.

GIBSON SHIPPING TOTALS for 'SG/Les Paul' Junior models: **1961** 2151 (includes some Les Paul Junior models); **1962** 2395; **1963** 2318 (includes some SG Junior models).

85

'SG/LES PAUL' STANDARD

1961-63 Bevelled-edge two-cutaway body; two humbucker pickups.
■ Bound rosewood fingerboard, crown markers; crown inlay on headstock; 'Les Paul' on truss-rod cover; plastic tuner buttons.
■ Bevelled-edge two-cutaway body; cherry.
■ Two metal-cover humbucker pickups.
■ Four controls (two volume, two tone) plus three-way selector; jack socket on body face.
■ Black laminated plastic pickguard.
■ Six-saddle bridge plus separate sideways-action vibrato tailpiece.
Some examples with standard-action vibrato tailpieces, some of which have inlaid decorative block in body face masking holes intended for sideways-action vibrato unit. Some examples in white or sunburst. Some examples with 'Les Paul Model' on headstock.

GIBSON SHIPPING TOTALS for 'SG/Les Paul' Standard models: **1961** 1662; **1962** 1449; **1963** 1445 (includes some SG Standard models).

SIGNATURE

1974-78 Semi-acoustic with two f-holes and offset cutaways.
■ Bound rosewood fingerboard, crown markers; 'Les Paul Signature' on headstock; plastic tuner buttons.
■ Bound semi-acoustic thinline body with two f-holes and offset cutaways; gold or sunburst.
■ Two rectangular plastic-cover low-impedance humbucker pickups.
■ Two controls (volume, tone) plus three-position impedance rotary switch, two-way phase rotary switch, and three-way selector; one jack socket on side of body for normal high-impedance output, plus second jack socket on body face for low-impedance output; built-in impedance transformer.
■ Cream plastic pickguard.
■ Six-saddle bridge plus separate bar tailpiece.
Earliest examples with two round-end

plastic-cover low-impedance humbucker pickups, and two side-mounted jack sockets.

GIBSON SHIPPING TOTALS for Signature models: **1973** 3; **1974** 1046; **1975** 118; **1976** 150; **1977** 123; **1978** 20; **1979** 3.

SIGNATURE BASS

1974-79 Semi-acoustic bass with two f-holes and offset cutaways.
■ Unbound rosewood fingerboard, crown markers; 34.5in scale, 20 frets; 'Les Paul Signature' on headstock.
■ Bound semi-acoustic thinline body with two f-holes and offset cutaways; gold top or sunburst.
■ One rectangular plastic-cover low-impedance humbucker pickup.
■ Two controls (volume, tone) plus three-position impedance rotary switch; one jack socket on side of body for normal high-impedance output, plus second jack socket on body face for low-impedance output; built-in impedance transformer.
■ Cream plastic pickguard.
■ Four-saddle bridge/tailpiece.
Earliest examples with one round-end plastic-cover low-impedance humbucker pickup, and two side-mounted jack sockets.

GIBSON SHIPPING TOTALS for Signature Bass models: **1973** 3; **1974** 428; **1975** 26; **1976** 44; **1977** 45; **1978** 23; **1979** 58.

SPECIAL

NORMAL MODELS chronological order

'SINGLE-CUT' *1955-58 Slab single-cutaway body, two pickups.*
■ Bound rosewood fingerboard, dot markers; 'Les Paul Special' on headstock; plastic tuner buttons.
■ Unbound slab body; beige.
■ Two plastic-cover six-polepiece single-coil pickups.
■ Four controls (two volume, two tone) plus three-way selector.

■ Black laminated plastic pickguard.
■ Wrap-over bar bridge/tailpiece.
Some early examples with brown plastic parts (knobs, pickguard etc).

'DOUBLE-CUT' *1959 Slab double-cutaway body, two pickups.*
■ Bound rosewood fingerboard, dot markers; 'Les Paul Special' on headstock; plastic tuner buttons.
■ Unbound slab double-cutaway body; yellow or cherry.
■ Two plastic-cover six-polepiece single-coil pickups.
■ Four controls (two volume, two tone) plus three-way selector.
■ Black laminated plastic pickguard.
■ Wrap-over bar bridge/tailpiece.
Later examples with neck pickup moved further down body, away from end of fingerboard; selector moved next to bridge (see p22/23).
Model name changed to SG Special in 1959 when Les Paul logo removed.

'DOUBLE-CUT THREE-QUARTER' *1959 Shorter 19-fret neck.*
Similar to 'DOUBLE-CUT' except:
■ Shorter neck (with 19 frets) and scale-length (2in less than normal).
■ Cherry finish only.
Model name changed to SG Special 3/4 in 1959 when Les Paul logo removed.

GIBSON SHIPPING TOTALS for Special models: **1955** 373; **1956** 1345; **1957** 1452; **1958** 958; **1959** 1821 (includes some SG Special models). And for Special 3/4 models: **1959** 12 (includes some SG Special 3/4 models).

OTHER SPECIAL MODELS alphabetical order

'55' *1974 & 77-80 Based on 'SINGLE-CUT': earliest examples with wrap-over bar bridge/tailpiece; majority have six-saddle bridge plus separate bar tailpiece. Sunbursts or colors. Earlier examples have plastic tuner buttons.*

GIBSON SHIPPING TOTALS for 'Special 55' models made at Kalamazoo: **1974** 1925; **1976** 2; **1977** 331; **1978** 293; **1979** 224.

Figures not available for 1980, nor for any Nashville production.

'58' 1976-79 *Based on 'DOUBLE-CUT' but six-saddle bridge plus separate bar tailpiece; sunbursts or colors.*

GIBSON SHIPPING TOTALS for 'Special 58' models made at Kalamazoo: **1976** 162; **1977** 1622; **1978** 803; **1979** 150. Figures not available for any Nashville production.

'SINGLE-CUT RE-ISSUE' 1988-current Similar to 'SINGLE-CUT', except:
■ Metal tuner buttons.
■ Sunburst, cherry, yellow or black.
■ Pickups, although visually similar to originals, are actually humbuckers.
■ Six-saddle bridge plus separate bar tailpiece.
Originally and erroneously referred to in Gibson literature as 'Junior II.'

SPOTLIGHT SPECIAL

1983 *Contrasting wood stripe down center of body.*
■ Bound rosewood fingerboard, crown markers; 'Les Paul Model' on headstock; 'Custom Shop Edition' logo on rear of headstock; '83' plus three-figure number on back of headstock instead of normal serial number; plastic tuner buttons.
■ Bound carved-top body with darker contrasting wood stripe down center; natural or sunburst.
■ Two metal-cover humbucker pickups.
■ Four controls (two volume, two tone) plus three-way selector.
■ No pickguard.
■ Six-saddle bridge plus separate bar tailpiece.
■ Gold-plated hardware.

STANDARD

1976-current 'Standard' on truss-rod cover.
■ Bound rosewood fingerboard, crown markers; 'Les Paul Model' on headstock; 'Standard' on truss-rod cover.

■ Bound carved-top body; sunbursts, natural or colors.
■ Two metal-cover humbucker pickups.
■ Four controls (two volume, two tone) plus three-way selector.
■ Cream plastic pickguard.
■ Six-saddle bridge plus separate bar tailpiece.
Also Standard Birdseye version (1993-current) with special figured maple top.
Also natural version with gold-plated hardware (1992-current).
For 1950s sunburst model, often referred to as 'Standard', see later 'SUNBURST' entry. For 1950s/1960s gold-top model, sometimes referred to as 'Standard', see earlier 'GOLD-TOP' entry.
For early 1960s SG-shaped version, see earlier 'SG/LES PAUL' STANDARD entry.
For 1980s STANDARD-80 models, see earlier HERITAGE SERIES entry.

GIBSON SHIPPING TOTALS for Standard models made at Kalamazoo: **1975** 1; **1976** 24; **1977** 586; **1978** 5947; **1979** 1054. Figures not available for large Nashville production started in 1970s, nor for 1980s & 1990s.

STUDIO

STUDIO 1983-current 'Studio' on truss-rod cover.
■ Unbound rosewood fingerboard (rosewood or ebony from 1986), dot markers (crown markers from 1990); 'Les Paul Model' on headstock; 'Studio' on truss-rod cover; plastic tuner buttons (metal from 1990).
■ Unbound carved-top body; sunburst, natural or colors.
■ Two metal-cover humbucker pickups.
■ Four controls (two volume, two tone) plus three-way selector.
■ Cream or laminated black plastic pickguard.
■ Six-saddle bridge plus separate bar tailpiece; optional bridge/vibrato unit.
■ Optional gold-plated hardware (from 1986).

STUDIO STANDARD 1984-87 Similar to STUDIO, except:

■ Bound fingerboard.
■ Bound carved-top body.

STUDIO CUSTOM 1984-85 Similar to STUDIO STANDARD, except:
■ Gold-plated hardware.

STUDIO LITE

'FIRST VERSION' 1988-90 *Unbound ebony fingerboard, dot markers.*
■ Unbound ebony fingerboard, dot markers; crown inlay on headstock.
■ Unbound carved-top thinner body with contoured back; sunbursts or colors.
■ Two plastic-cover humbucker pickups.
■ Two controls (volume, tone) plus three-way selector and mini-switch.
■ No pickguard.
■ Six-saddle bridge plus separate bar tailpiece; optional bridge/vibrato unit (1988-89).
■ Black-plated or gold-plated hardware.

'SECOND VERSION' 1990-current *Unbound ebony fingerboard, crown markers.* Similar to 'FIRST VERSION', except:
■ Crown markers.
■ 'Les Paul Model' on headstock.
■ Lightweight carved-top flat-back body.
■ Two coverless humbucker pickups.
■ Two volumes, two tones, three-way selector.
Also version with three-piece figured maple top, amber or red (1991).

STUDIO LITE/MIII 1992-current Similar to 'SECOND VERSION', except:
■ Two coverless humbuckers plus one central six-polepiece single-coil pickup.
■ Two controls (volume, tone) plus five-way selector and mini-switch.

'SUNBURST'

1958-60 Similar to 'GOLD-TOP FOURTH VERSION' (see listing in earlier 'GOLD-TOP' section), except:
■ Body with sunburst top.

88

GIBSON SHIPPING TOTALS for 'Sunburst' models: **1958** 434 (includes some 'Gold-top' models); **1959** 643; **1960** 635.

OTHER 'SUNBURST' MODELS
CMT 1986-89 *Similar to '59 RE-ISSUE' except wide binding in cutaway, metal jack-socket plate. Stands for 'curly maple top.'*

'59 RE-ISSUE' 1985-current *Based on 1959-period original.*

'60 RE-ISSUE' 1992-current *Based on 1960-period original, ie slimmer neck profile.*

THE LES PAUL

1976-79 *'The Les Paul' on truss-rod cover.*
■ Bound ebony fingerboard, block markers; split-diamond inlay on head-stock; 'The Les Paul' on truss-rod cover; plastic tuner buttons.
■ Bound carved-top body; natural or red.
■ Two metal-cover humbucker pickups.
■ Four controls (two volume, two tone) plus three-way selector.
■ Wooden pickguard.
■ Six-saddle bridge plus separate bar tailpiece.
■ Gold-plated hardware.
Some examples with fine-tuning tailpiece. Most examples have carved wooden components (pickup surrounds, pickguard, knobs etc) rather than plastic.

GIBSON SHIPPING TOTALS for The Les Paul models: **1976** 33; **1977** 10; **1979** 11. Figures not available for 1978.

TRIUMPH BASS

See earlier LES PAUL BASS entry, under 'SECOND VERSION'.

TV

'SINGLE-CUT' 1955-58 *Slab single-cutaway body, one pickup, beige finish, 'Les Paul TV Model' on headstock.*
■ Unbound rosewood fingerboard, dot

markers; 'Les Paul TV Model' on headstock; plastic tuner buttons.
■ Unbound slab body; beige.
■ One plastic-cover six-polepiece single-coil pickup.
■ Two controls (volume, tone).
■ Black or tortoiseshell plastic pickguard.
■ Wrap-over bar bridge/tailpiece.
A 'three-quarter' short-scale version has been documented.

'DOUBLE-CUT' 1958-59 *Slab double-cutaway body, one pickup, yellow finish, 'Les Paul TV Model' on headstock.*
■ Unbound rosewood fingerboard, dot markers; 'Les Paul TV Model' on headstock; plastic tuner buttons.
■ Unbound slab double-cutaway body; yellow.
■ One plastic-cover six-polepiece single-coil pickup.
■ Two controls (volume, tone).
■ Black or tortoiseshell plastic pickguard.
■ Wrap-over bar bridge/tailpiece.
Name changed to SG TV in 1959 when Les Paul logo removed.

GIBSON SHIPPING TOTALS for TV models: **1954** 5; **1955** 230; **1956** 511; **1957** 552; **1958** 429; **1959** 543 (includes some SG TV models).

20th ANNIVERSARY

CUSTOM 20TH ANNIVERSARY 1974
Anniversary model based on CUSTOM 'THIRD VERSION' (see listing in earlier CUSTOM section) but with 'Twentieth Anniversary' inlaid into position marker at 15th fret. Sunburst or colors.

25/50 ANNIVERSARY

1978-79 *'25 50' inlay on headstock.*
■ Bound ebony fingerboard, split-block markers; 'Les Paul 25 50' on headstock; 'Les Paul Anniversary' on gold-plated metal truss-rod cover; brass nut; four-figure number on back of headstock in addition to normal serial number.

■ Bound carved-top body; sunburst, natural, red or black.
■ Two metal-cover humbucker pickups.
■ Four controls (two volume, two tone) plus three-way selector and mini-switch.
■ Black laminated plastic pickguard.
■ Six-saddle bridge plus separate bar tailpiece with six fine-tuning knobs.
■ Gold-/chrome-plated hardware.

GIBSON SHIPPING TOTALS for 25/50 Anniversary models: **1978** 1106; **1979** 2305.

30th ANNIVERSARY

'GOLD-TOP' 30th ANNIVERSARY 1982-83 *Anniversary model based on 'GOLD-TOP FOURTH VERSION' (see listing in earlier 'GOLD-TOP' section) but with 'Thirtieth Anniversary' inlaid into position marker at 19th fret.*

'SG/LES PAUL' CUSTOM 30th ANNIVERSARY 1991-92 *Anniversary model based on 'SG/LES PAUL CUSTOM RE-ISSUE' (see listing in earlier 'SG/LES PAUL' CUSTOM section) but split-diamond inlay on headstock has '30th Anniversary' in bar and '1961, 1991' in diamond sections. Yellow finish.*

35th ANNIVERSARY

35th ANNIVERSARY 1989-90 *Anniversary model based on CUSTOM 'SECOND VERSION' (see listing in earlier CUSTOM section) but with '35th Anniversary' in bar of split-diamond inlay on headstock.*

40th ANNIVERSARY

1991-current *Similar to 'GOLD-TOP THIRD VERSION' (see listing in earlier 'GOLD-TOP' section) except:*
■ Ebony fingerboard; '40th Anniversary' inlaid into position marker at 12th fret and on rear of headstock.
■ Black finish.
■ Pickups, although visually similar, are actually humbuckers.
■ Gold-plated hardware.

MODELS & YEARS	
'GOLD-TOP' 1st version (long trapeze)	1952-53
'GOLD-TOP' 2nd version (angled 1-piece bridge)	1953-55
CUSTOM 1st version (black pickups)	1954-57
JUNIOR 'SINGLE-CUT'	1954-58
TV 'SINGLE-CUT'	1955-58
'GOLD-TOP' 3rd version (white p/ups; 6-sadd bridge)	1955-57
SPECIAL 'SINGLE-CUT'	1955-58
JUNIOR 'SINGLE-CUT THREE-QUARTER'	1956-58
'GOLD-TOP' 4th version (humbuckers)	1957-58
CUSTOM 2nd version (3 humbuckers)	1957-61
TV 'DOUBLE-CUT'	1958-59
'SUNBURST'	1958-60
JUNIOR 'DOUBLE-CUT'	1958-61
JUNIOR 'DOUBLE-CUT THREE-QUARTER'	1958-61
SPECIAL 'DOUBLE-CUT'	1959
SPECIAL 'DOUBLE-CUT THREE-QUARTER'	1959
'SG/LES PAUL' CUSTOM	1961-63
'SG/LES PAUL' JUNIOR	1961-63
'SG/LES PAUL' STANDARD	1961-63
'GOLD-TOP' 5th version (6-sadd bridge; sep t/piece)	1968-69
CUSTOM 3rd version (2 humbuckers)	1968-current
BASS 1st version (most controls not on panel)	1969-70
PROFESSIONAL	1969-71
PERSONAL	1969-72
DELUXE	1969-84
JUMBO	1970-71
'GOLD-TOP' 6th version (angled 1-piece bridge)	1971-72
RECORDING 1st version (all controls on panel)	1971-77
TRIUMPH BASS (BASS 2nd ver'n: all controls on panel)	1971-79
CUSTOM '54 LTD EDITION'	1972-73
CUSTOM 20TH ANNIVERSARY	1974
SIGNATURE	1974-78
SIGNATURE BASS	1974-79
SPECIAL 55 (single-cut)	1974, 77-80
THE LES PAUL	1976-79
SPECIAL 58 (double-cut)	1976-79
PRO DELUXE	1976-82
STANDARD	1976-current
ARTISAN 1st version (three pickups)	1977-79
RECORDING 2nd version (selector by neck pickup)	1977-79
25/50 ANNIVERSARY	1978-79
ARTISAN 2nd version (two pickups)	1978-82
KM	1979
ARTIST	1979-81
HERITAGE STANDARD 80	1980-82
HERITAGE STANDARD 80 ELITE	1980-82
LP XRI	1981-82
LP XRII	1981-82
LP XRIII	1982
'GOLD-TOP' 30th ANNIVERSARY	1982-83
SPOTLIGHT SPECIAL	1983
STUDIO	1983-current
STUDIO CUSTOM	1984-85
STUDIO STANDARD	1984-87
'GOLD-TOP 57 RE-ISSUE' (humbuckers)	1985-current
'SUNBURST 59 RE-ISSUE'	1985-current
JUNIOR 58 (double-cut)	1986-87
'SUNBURST' CMT	1986-89
JUNIOR 54 (single-cut)	1986-91
CUSTOM LITE	1987-89
'SG/LES PAUL' CUSTOM re-issue	1987-90
STUDIO LITE 1st version (dot markers)	1988-90
SPECIAL 'SINGLE-CUT' re-issue ('Junior II')	1988-current
35th ANNIVERSARY	1989-90
'GOLD-TOP 56 RE-ISSUE' (white pickups)	1989-current
CLASSIC	1990-current
STUDIO LITE 2nd version (crown markers)	1990-current
CLASSIC/MIII	1991-92
'SG/LES PAUL' CUSTOM 30th ANNIVERSARY	1991-92
40th ANNIVERSARY	1991-current
CLASSIC CELEBRITY	1992
CLASSIC PLUS	1992-current
CUSTOM BLACK BEAUTY 54	1992-current
CUSTOM BLACK BEAUTY 57 (2 pickups)	1992-current
CUSTOM BLACK BEAUTY 57 (3 pickups)	1992-current
CUSTOM PLUS	1992-current
CUSTOM/400	1992-current
DELUXE re-issue	1992-current
DELUXE BASS	1992-current
SPECIAL BASS	1992-current
STANDARD BASS	1992-current
STUDIO LITE/MIII	1992-current
'SUNBURST 60 RE-ISSUE' (slim neck)	1992-current
CLASSIC BIRDSEYE	1993-current
CLASSIC PREMIUM PLUS	1993-current
CLASSIC PREMIUM BIRDSEYE	1993-current
CUSTOM PREMIUM PLUS	1993-current
DELUXE PLUS BASS	1993-current
DELUXE PREMIUM PLUS BASS	1993-current
STANDARD PLUS BASS	1993-current
STANDARD PREMIUM PLUS BASS	1993-current

89

DATING GIBSON LES PAULS

It is both satisfying and important to determine the production date of an instrument. If a guitar can be accurately assigned to a specific period then the owner is able to relate it to personal history or to relevant musical styles and famous players. Such associations do have significant bearing on value, and where Gibson Les Paul guitars are concerned the 'vintage' is definitely a prime aspect. In terms of perceived quality and performance capabilities, certain years are considered far more desirable than others, and so any clues that confirm an instrument's age are worthwhile and welcome.

In this book we are dealing with a comparatively small selection of guitars from the vast range of instruments produced by the Gibson company over a period of 40 years and more. Gibson instituted surprisingly few changes during this relatively lengthy production span that might enable a Les Paul owner easily and accurately to ascertain the age of an instrument.

It should be stressed here that no single dating method provides a foolproof conclusion regarding exact vintage. Gibson like all mass-manufacturers of instruments made numerous amendments to production procedures, construction routines and component styles. However, invariably many of these changes would be put into effect over a period of time, and not instantaneously. Often existing parts would continue to be used, sometimes in combination with revised methods or new features, thus creating a variety of 'transitional' guitars. Such instruments tend to cause confusion and blur the chronological picture. But by careful scrutiny of a number of aspects it should be possible to recognize and eliminate such potential pitfalls and date most Gibson Les Pauls to a relatively narrow time slot.

VINTAGE VERIFICATION

Instruments from Fender and other makers are often easier to date than those from Gibson, because guitars with the latter brand tend to yield fewer of the more obvious clues. Many that can be used often require direct comparison between two or more instruments, or involve technical measuring equipment or specialized knowledge of the construction and workings of Gibson's electric guitars. It is essential to have a keen, trained eye, plus a very good memory, as some aspects of the data relating to the age of Les Pauls are complex and confusing.

Just as with Fender and other high profile American-made brands, many Gibson instruments occupy prime positions in the 'vintage' market. Certain Les Pauls are among the most desirable, and therefore reside at the very top of the big-money league. Other Les Paul models command much interest and value, and the year of manufacture has a great bearing on prices, to the extent that this aspect has become over-emphasized. All too often 'vintage' assumes more importance than the inherent quality and playability of an individual guitar. Some Les Pauls therefore have very little appeal among players and collectors due to the poor regard in which a particular production period is held – and here, determining age helps in knowing what it is best to avoid.

Specific changes made to various Les Pauls have been included in the relevant entries in the preceding instrument listing. Such details do provide a more accurate timescale for individual models, but there are a number of more general indicators of age, and these are shown here. Of course, these are only of use if they are *original to the instrument concerned*. With so many broad similarities between groups of Les Paul models, even the switching of something as seemingly innocent as a truss-rod cover can give the impression that one model is actually another, even on relatively recent guitars. As usual, please beware of modifications made to mislead.

Note that 'c' in front of a date means 'circa,' or 'about.'

GIBSON HEADSTOCK LOGO

The Gibson brandname assumes pride of place on the headstock of all Les Pauls. The style and method of lettering has undergone various small changes over the years, and these can be related to certain periods. While many are extremely minor and can be very hard to spot or determine accurately, some are less subtle and of more immediate help.

From c1952 to c1968 the dot of the 'i' in 'Gibson' was not joined to the 'G,' and the 'b' and 'o' were not continuously solid.

From c1968 the 'i' lost its dot, and the 'b' and 'o' became continuously solid.

In 1972 the dotted 'i' appeared again, but then came and went with confusing irregularity until c1981.

From 1981 the 'o' and 'n' were linked at the top, and not at the bottom as usually seen. However, the latter style was soon reintroduced, and the two versions have been used ever since.

HEADSTOCK ANGLE

From 1965 to 1973 the tilt angle of the headstock in relation to the neck was altered from a previously standardized 17 degrees to 14 degrees. In 1973 the angle of 17 degrees was re-introduced, but both have been employed since. Direct comparison between two instruments is necessary to determine the rather subtle difference of three degrees.

HEADSTOCK 'VOLUTE'

A 'volute' is a carved 'heel' situated at the transition point between the rear of the neck and the angled headstock. The extra timber was intended to provide reinforcement in this potentially weak area. Gibson introduced the feature c1970, and kept it until about 1981.

'MADE IN USA' HEADSTOCK LOGO

From 1970 to 1975 'Made In USA' was stamped into the rear of the headstock. A version of this logo on a transfer was applied from 1975 to 1977, but in 1977 the stamping method was reintroduced and has continued ever since.

GIBSON PICKUP LOGO
Plastic-covered P90 and metal-covered humbucker pickups carried the Gibson logo from c1970 to c1972.

CONTROL KNOBS
Gibson has employed five distinct types of control knob on the Les Paul models over the years, and these do help to indicate production periods, although of course certain versions have since been re-introduced. The dates shown below refer to the original periods of use.

'SPEED' KNOB Smooth-side 'barrel' shape, internal numbers, clear/colored all-plastic. First used c1952 to c1955.

'BELL' KNOB Smooth-side 'bell' shape, internal numbers, clear/colored all-plastic. First used c1955 to c1960.

'METAL TOP' KNOB Smooth-side larger 'bell' shape, internal numbers, clear/colored plastic with 'Volume' or 'Tone' on inset large metal top. First used c1960 to c1967.

'WITCH HAT' KNOB Ribbed-side conical shape, numbered skirt, black plastic with 'Volume' or 'Tone' on small metal top. First used c1967 to c1975.

CONTROL POT CODES
Removing the back control plate on Les Pauls will reveal the metal casings of the control potentiometers (usually called 'pots'). Many American-made pot casings carry code numbers which, when translated, provide a useful confirmation of the instrument's age. However, note that: (a) coded pots were not always used immediately; and (b) pots may subsequently have been replaced. The code comprises six or seven digits. The first three identify the manufacturer and can be ignored. The next one or two digits show the year: one shows the last digit of 195X; a pair indicates any year thereafter. The final two digits signify the week of the appropriate year.

BRIDGE
Gibson has used various types of bridges on Les Paul models since 1952. Some have been re-introduced since their first appearances; the dates shown below refer to the original periods of use.

'WRAP-UNDER' Combination unit with two long rod 'anchors,' as on the very first Les Paul gold-tops. First used 1952 to 1953.

'WRAP-OVER' Stud-mounted successor to the above. First used 1953 to c1962.

'RIDGED WRAP-OVER' As the previous unit, but with a staggered, moulded ridge on the top. First used c1962 to c1971.

'TUNE-O-MATIC' A bridge with six saddles, individually adjustable for length. First used c1954 to c1961.

'TUNE-O-MATIC RETAINER' As above, but with a bridge-saddle retaining wire. First used c1961 to c1971.

'TUNE-O-MATIC NYLON' As above, but with white nylon bridge saddles replacing the metal type of the other versions. First used c1961 to c1971.

'NEW TUNE-O-MATIC' A heavier-duty version with no bridge-saddle retaining wire. Introduced c1971 and still in use.

'NASHVILLE' A large rectangular bridge with six long-travel metal saddles. First used c1971 to c1982.

SERIAL NUMBERS
Gibson has changed its system for serial numbering of instruments several times, and only certain periods provide logical and orderly sequences. In these instances it is easy to give an accurate production date to a guitar once the appropriate system is understood. However, the company has also been guilty of using numbers which appear to have little basis in logic, often being applied out of sequence or, worse still, duplicated once or more. Such numbers provide confusion and very little else, and

they should of course be disregarded for dating purposes (except perhaps to confirm a broad period indicated by clues from construction styles and component types).

The earliest Les Paul gold-tops had no serial numbers, but as production increased some examples were assigned a three-digit number stamped on the top edge of the headstock.

In 1953 a serial numbering system was instituted specifically for the new Gibson solidbodies. This initially comprised a five-digit number, ink-stamped onto the rear of the headstock. The first digit was slightly apart from the other four and signified the year of manufacture. In 1955 increased output necessitated the addition of a sixth digit (located after the date code) to some sequences. In both styles, the first digit provides the date: 3 = 1953;

$$4 = 1954;$$
$$5 = 1955;$$
$$6 = 1956;$$
$$7 = 1957;$$
$$8 = 1958;$$
$$9 = 1959;$$
$$0 = 1960.$$

During 1961 inked-on numbering was replaced by a method using digits actually stamped into the back of the headstock. At this time Gibson introduced a new serialization system for all instruments. These numbers were supposed to be allocated in a strict sequence, but this didn't happen in practice — and the fun started. Many instruments from the 1960s carry duplicated serial numbers, used not only twice but sometimes as many as six or seven times on different guitars.

Similar problems afflicted manufacture for the first five years of the 1970s, with numerous duplications of sequences appearing on both 1960s and 1970s guitars. It is extremely difficult to provide a useful table of the numbers used during this 15-year period, and any listing (see overleaf) will provide only a very approximate guide, mainly serving to indicate some of the duplicated permutations.

91

The tables of serial numbers (here and opposite page) give a rough guide to some of the sequences that Gibson used (and duplicated) between 1961 and 1975. The serial number series are broken down into thousands or groups of thousands, where '100,000s', for example, means 100,001 to 199,999, or more specifically something like '438,000s' means 438,001 to 438,999. The dates shown next to the sequences are approximate, and can only really be used to confirm a broad period already indicated by more solid clues from the model type of the guitar in question, its construction style and the components it uses.

SERIAL NUMBERS 1961-1975

Number series	Circa
100 to 61,000s	1961-62
61,000s to 70,000s	1962-64
71,000s to 99,000s	1962-63
000,000s	1967, 1973-75
100,000s	1963-67, 1970-75
100,000s to 144,000s	1963-64, 1967
147,000s to 199,000s	1963-65
200,000s to 290,000s	1964-65, 1973-75
300,000s	1965-68, 1974-75
301,000s to 305,000s	1965
306,000s to 307,000s	1965, 1967
309,000s to 310,000s	1965, 1967
311,000s to 326,000s	1965, 1967
328,000s to 329,000s	1965
329,000s to 332,000s	1965, 1967-68
332,000s to 368,000s	1965-66
368,000s to 370,000s	1966-67
380,000s to 385,000s	1966
390,000s	1967
400,000s	1965-68, 1974-75
401,000s to 409,000s	1966
420,000s to 438,000s	1966
500,000s	1965-66, 1968-69, 1974-75
501,000s to 503,000s	1965
501,000s to 530,000s	1968
530,000s	1966
530,000s to 545,000s	1969
540,000s	1966
550,000s to 556,000s	1966
558,000s to 567,000s	1969

SERIAL NUMBERS 1961-1975

Number series	Circa
570,000s	1966
580,000s	1969
600,000s	1966-69, 1970-72, 1974-75
601,000s	1969
605,000s to 606,000s	1969
700,000s	1966-67, 1970-72
750,000s	1968-69
800,000s	1966-69, 1973-75
801,000s to 812,000s	1966, 1969
812,000s to 814,000s	1969
817,000s to 819,000s	1969
820,000s	1969
820,000s to 823,000s	1966
824,000s	1969
828,000s to 847,000s	1966, 1969
847,000s to 858,000s	1966
859,000s to 880,000s	1967
893,000s to 897,000s	1967
895,000s to 896,000s	1968
897,000s to 898,000s	1967
899,000s to 920,000s	1968
900,000s	1968, 1970-72
940,000s to 943,000s	1968
945,000s	1968
947,000s to 966,000s	1968
970,000s to 972,000s	1968
A + 6 digits	1973-75
B, C, D, E or F + 6 digits	1974-75

In 1975 Gibson at last replaced their previous haphazard system with a much simpler scheme, which ran for three years. This used eight digits, the first two of which formed a coded date prefix: 99 = 1975; 00 = 1976; 06 = 1977. And instead of being stamped into the back of the headstock, serial numbers from this series were part of a transfer which also included the model name and 'Made In USA.'

In 1977 Gibson reverted to stamping the serial number into the rear of the headstock, and changed the serial number system yet again. The number remained at eight digits, but now the first and fifth indicated the year of production. For example, 93291369 indicates a model produced in 1991. This system has proved to be successful and reliable, and is still in operation at the time of writing.

The various methods and systems of serial numbering outlined here cover most Gibson Les Pauls issued between 1952 and 1993. However, there are various unusual series, special prefixes and so on which are found on instruments coming from the Custom Shop, on limited editions, vintage re-issue models and others. As these are only relevant to specific models and offer no overall dating assistance, they have been excluded from this listing (but may sometimes be found mentioned elsewhere in the text).

On some instruments made by Gibson a separate stamped '2' can be seen, usually below the serial number, and this indicates a factory 'second.' This is an instrument officially identified at some point in its production as having some cosmetic defect, usually minor and often very hard to detect.

OWNERS' CREDITS

Guitars photographed came from the following individuals' collections, and we are grateful for their help. The owners at the time of photography are listed here in the alphabetical order of the code used to identify their guitars in the Photographic Index below: **AR** Alan Rogan; **ARA** Arthur Ramm; **BB** Bruce Bowling; **CB** Clive Brown; **DN** David Noble; **GH** George Harrison; **GJ** Ged Johnson; **GMA** Garry Malone; **GMO** Gary Moore; **GUK** Gibson UK (Consolidated Musical Instruments, London); **GUS** Gibson USA; **HK** Hiroshi Kato; **JB** Jeff Beck; **JC** John Coleman; **JP** Jimmy Page; **JS** John Smith; **MN** Marc Noel-Johnson (Music Village); **MW** Mick Watts (Music Unlimited); **NB** Nick Briers (Abbey Road Music); **NS** Nick Sattin; **PD** Paul Day; **RH** Rick Harrison (Music Ground); **SC** Simon Carlton; **SH** Shane's; **SJ** Scott Jennings (Route 66 Guitars USA); **TA** Terry Anthony.

PHOTOGRAPHIC INDEX

Our main photographer was Nigel Bradley, of Visuel 7. Additional pictures were taken by Garth Blore, Billy Mitchell and Mitch Tobias. Thanks also to Gruhn Guitars for supplying two existing photographs, to Will Taylor at Visuel 7, and to Scott Jennings for a photograph at short notice.

Under the relevant page number is a brief identification of each guitar shown, followed by the owner's initials in bold letters (as listed in the Owners Credits above). For example '6: Sunburst AR' means that the Sunburst model pictured on page 6 was owned by Alan Rogan.

Jacket front: 1957 Gold-top **DN**. *Jacket back:* 1992 'Jimmy Wallace' 59 Re-issue lefty **JC**. 6: Sunburst **AR**. 10: gold-top **JS**; Custom **DN**. 11: gold-top lefty **TA**; gold-top detail **GJ**. 14-15: Junior **DN**; Special **DN**. 15: TV **CB**. 18-19: Custom **DN**; gold-top **DN**. 19: Gold-top detail **JS**. 22: Special ³⁄₄ **SH**. 22-23: Junior **CB**; Special lefty **SJ**. 26-27: All **JP**. 30-31: **JB**, **GMO**, as noted. 34-35: **GH**, **ARA**, as noted. 38-39: Custom **DN**; Standard **DN**. 39: Junior **SC**. 42: gold-top **MN**. 43: Deluxe **NS**; 1980 detail **BB**; Custom **JS**. 46-47: Personal **HK**; Signature **GMA**. 47: Recording **PD**; Signature Bass **RH**. 50-51: The Les Paul **GMA**; Pro Deluxe SC. 51: Artisan

GMA; 20th **NB**; 25/50 **GMA**. 54-55: Heritage **MW**; Spotlight **GMA**. 55: Standard **SC**; Artist **GMA**. 58: 59 Re-issue **DN**; Hollow **AR**. 59: 35th **DN**; Samurai **GUS**; Studio Lite **GMA**. 62: Custom Plus **RH**. 62-63: Deluxe Bass **GUK**. 63: 40th **JC**; Standard **SC**; Studio Lite/MIII **GUK**.

MEMORABILIA including catalogs, brochures and photographs came from the collections of Tony Bacon, Jamie Crompton, Paul Day, Ted McCarty, Alan Rogan and Steve Soest, photographed by Tony Bacon (with thanks to Will Taylor of Visuel 7).

IN ADDITION to those named above in Owners' Credits, we would also like to thank: Chris Albano (Hal Leonard); Kent Armstrong; Ralph Baker (Equator Music); Ian Bishop (IMP); Bruce Bolen (Fender Musical Instruments, Nashville); Julie Bowie; Craig Bradley (Craig's Music); Dave Burrluck (*The Guitar Magazine*); Carter (Jimmy Page); Walter Carter; Doug Chandler & Paula Chandler (Chandler Guitars); Betty Clinch & Sharon Clinch; Roger Cooper (Balafon); Jamie Crompton (Consolidated Musical Instruments, London); Merelyn Davis; Jane, Sarah & Simon Day; Ralph Denyer; Jim Deurloo (Heritage Guitar Inc); André Duchossoir; Paul Fischer; Roger Giffin (Gibson West Coast Custom Shop); Brian Good (Outrider Management); Justin Harrison (Music Ground); Richard Head (Gibson Guitar Corp); Skip Henderson (City Lights Music); Steve Hopkins (Hopkins Musical Instruments); Terri Horak (*Billboard*); Steve Hoyland; Adrian Ingram; Henry Juskiewicz (Gibson Guitar Corp); Matt Kelsey (Miller Freeman); Dave Kenton (IMP); Jo Killeen & Eddie Bull (Gelfand Rennert & Feldman); Marv Lamb (Heritage Guitar Inc); Mel Lambert; Jon Lewin & Paul Quinn (*Making Music*); Graham Lilley (Part Rock Management); Adrian Lovegrove; Seth Lover & Lavone Lover; Neville Marten (*Music Maker Publications*); Gareth Malone; Ted McCarty (Bigsby Accessories Inc); J P Moats (Heritage Guitar Inc); Lee-Ellen Newman (East West Records); Stuart Palmer (Music Ground); Les Paul; Peter Pulham (Music Business); Ian Purser; Stan Rendell; J T Riboloff (Gibson Guitar Corp); Paul Rodgers; Cynthia Roorbach (Bigsby Accessories Inc);

David Seville (Yamaha Music Ltd); Tim Shaw (Bellevue Guitar Repair); Dorothy Smith; Steve Soest (Soest Guitar Repair); David Sumner; Paul Trynka (United Leisure Magazines); Jerry Uwins (UMS); Adrian Walker (Making Music Ltd); Lew Weston.

SPECIAL THANKS to Steve Soest and family – Paula, Amy, Amber and Jesse Ray – for hospitality and Hallowe'en.

UNSOURCED QUOTATIONS in the text are taken from original interviews with Bruce Bolen, Jim Deurloo, Henry Juskiewicz, Marv Lamb, Seth Lover, Ted McCarty, J P Moats, Les Paul, Stan Rendell, J T Riboloff and Tim Shaw, conducted by Tony Bacon between October 1992 and March 1993, and from an interview with Les Paul conducted by Tony Bacon in March 1989 (for a feature in *Making Music* magazine). The sources of previously published quotations are given where they occur in the text.

BOOKS consulted during research include: Tony Bacon & Paul Day *The Fender Book* (GPI 1992), *The Ultimate Guitar Book* (Knopf 1991), *The Guru's Guitar Guide* (Bold Strummer 1990/1992); John Bulli *Guitar History Volume 2* (Bold Strummer 1989); André Duchossoir *Gibson Electrics Volume 1* (Mediapresse 1981), *Guitar Identification* (Hal Leonard 1990); George Gruhn & Walter Carter *Gruhn's Guide to Vintage Guitars* (GPI 1991); Guitar Magazine 'Mooks' *The Gibson* (Rittor 1992); Albert Jackson & David Day *Collins Good Wood Handbook* (HarperCollins 1991); Colin Larkin (ed) *The Guinness Encyclopedia of Popular Music* (Guinness 1992); Stephen K Peeples *Les Paul: The Legend and the Legacy* – booklet with CD box-set (Capitol 1991); Thomas A Van Hoose *The Gibson Super 400* (GPI 1991); Tom Wheeler *American Guitars* (HarperPerennial 1990).

We also used for research various back issues of the following magazines: *Beat Instrumental; Billboard; Disc International; Gibson Gazette; Guitar Player; Guitar World; Making Music; Melody Maker; Music Trades; Music World; One Two Testing.*

To my dad, for 'Les Paul Now' and much more besides – TB

96